THE 2006 LEBANON CAMPAIGN AND THE FUTURE OF WARFARE: IMPLICATIONS FOR ARMY AND DEFENSE POLICY

Stephen Biddle
Jeffrey A. Friedman

September 2008

*****

The views expressed in this report are those of the authors and do not necessarily reflect the official policy or position of the Department of the Army, the Department of Defense, or the U.S. Government. This report is cleared for public release; distribution is unlimited.

*****

Comments pertaining to this report are invited and should be forwarded to: Director, Strategic Studies Institute, U.S. Army War College, 122 Forbes Ave, Carlisle, PA 17013-5244.

*****

The Strategic Studies Institute publishes a monthly e-mail newsletter to update the national security community on the research of our analysts, recent and forthcoming publications, and upcoming conferences sponsored by the Institute. Each newsletter also provides a strategic commentary by one of our research analysts. If you are interested in receiving this newsletter, please subscribe on our homepage at *www.StrategicStudiesInstitute.army. mil/newsletter/.*

ISBN 978-1-257-12878-5

ACKNOWLEDGMENTS

The authors would like to thank the many individuals whose comments on previous drafts or briefings have improved the final monograph, and particularly Nir Artzi, Andrew Exum, Thomas McNaugher, and Yuri Zhukov. The authors would also like to express their thanks to Brigadier General Itai Brun of the Israel Defense Force for his support and assistance in the field work on which the research is based; to BG Brun and the staff of the Dado Center for Interdisciplinary Military Studies of the Israel Defense Force for their thoughtful and energetic comments on interim project briefings; and to Mr. Martin Peled-Flax of the Israeli Embassy in Washington, Maj. Dan Fayutkin of the Dado Center, Dima Adamsky of Columbia University, and Lt. Moran Maymon, Private Elena Papageorghiou, and Private Maureen Shaldag of the IDF Spokesperson's office for their assistance in arranging interviews and base access in Israel. Nir Artzi provided critical research assistance in the Hebrew literature on the war, for which the authors are grateful. Finally, the authors would like to thank the thirty-six IDF officers whose interviews form the basis of the analysis presented here, and without whose generous contributions of time and cooperation this research would not have been possible. Any errors of fact or interpretation, of course, are the responsibility of the authors.

CONTENTS

FIGURES

FOREWORD

Hezbollah's conduct of its 2006 campaign in southern Lebanon has become an increasingly important case for the U.S. defense debate. Some see the future of warfare as one of nonstate opponents employing irregular methods, and advocate a sweeping transformation of the U.S. military to meet such threats. Others point to the 2006 campaign as an example of a nonstate actor nevertheless waging a state-like conventional war, and argue that a more traditional U.S. military posture is needed to deal with such enemies in the future.

This monograph, by Dr. Stephen Biddle of the Council on Foreign Relations and Mr. Jeffrey Friedman, Harvard Kennedy School of Government, seeks to inform this debate by examining in detail Hezbollah's conduct of the 2006 campaign. The authors use evidence collected from a series of 36 primary source interviews with Israeli participants in the fighting who were in a position to observe Hezbollah's actual behavior in the field in 2006, coupled with deductive inference from observable Hezbollah behavior in the field to findings for their larger strategic intent for the campaign.

The Strategic Studies Institute is pleased to offer this monograph as a contribution to the national security debate on this important topic.

DOUGLAS C. LOVELACE, JR.
Director
Strategic Studies Institute

BIOGRAPHICAL SKETCHES OF THE AUTHORS

STEPHEN BIDDLE is Senior Fellow for Defense Policy at the Council on Foreign Relations. Before joining the Council in January 2006, he held the Elihu Root Chair in Military Studies at the U.S. Army War College, Strategic Studies Institute (SSI), and has held teaching and research posts at the University of North Carolina at Chapel Hill; the Institute for Defense Analyses (IDA); Harvard University's Belfer Center for Science and International Affairs (BCSIA); and the Kennedy School of Government's Office of National Security Programs. His book, *Military Power: Explaining Victory and Defeat in Modern Battle* (Princeton University Press, 2004), has won four prizes, including the Council on Foreign Relations Arthur Ross Award Silver Medal for 2005, and the 2005 Huntington Prize from the Harvard University Olin Institute for Strategic Studies. His other publications include articles in *Foreign Affairs, International Security, Survival, The Journal of Politics, The Journal of Strategic Studies, The Journal of Conflict Resolution, Security Studies, Contemporary Security Policy, Defense Analysis,* and *Military Operations Research*; shorter pieces on military topics in *The National Interest, Orbis,* the *New York Times, The Washington Post,* the *Wall Street Journal, The Boston Globe, The International Herald Tribune, the Suddeutsche Zeitung, the Guardian, Joint Force Quarterly,* and *Defense News*; various chapters in edited volumes; and 29 IDA, SSI, MNF-I and NATO reports. Dr. Biddle has presented testimony before congressional committees on issues relating to the war in Iraq, conventional net assessment, and European arms control; served on the MNF-I Joint Strategic Assessment Team in Baghdad; served as U.S. Representative to the NATO Defense Research Group study on Stable Defense; is co-director of the Columbia University Summer Workshop on the Analysis of Military Operations and Strategy (SWAMOS); has served as a member of the Defense Department Senior Advisory Group on Homeland Defense; and holds an appointment as Adjunct Associate Professor of International and Public Affairs at Columbia University. Dr. Biddle holds AB (1981), MPP (1985), and Ph.D. (Public Policy, 1992) degrees, all from Harvard University.

JEFFREY A. FRIEDMAN is a doctoral student in public policy at the John F. Kennedy School of Government. From 2006 to 2008 he was Research Associate for Defense Policy at the Council on Foreign Relations in Washington, DC. He has held prior research positions at the World Bank and the John M. Olin Institute for Strategic Studies. Mr. Friedman holds a Bachelor's Degree in Government from Harvard College.

SUMMARY

The future of nonstate military actors is a central issue for U.S. strategy and defense planning. It is widely believed that such combatants will be increasingly common opponents for the U.S. military, and many now advocate sweeping change in U.S. military posture to prepare for this—the debate over the associated agenda for "low-tech" or irregular warfare transformation is quickly becoming one of the central issues for U.S. defense policy and strategy. As a prominent recent example of a nonstate actor fighting a Westernized state, Hezbollah's 2006 campaign thus offers a window into a kind of warfare that is increasingly central to the defense debate in the United States. And the case's implications for U.S. policy have already become highly controversial.

Some see Hezbollah as an essentially terrorist organization using an information age version of the asymmetric military methods seen as typical of nonstate actors historically. This view of Hezbollah as an information age guerrilla force strengthens the case for a major redesign of the U.S. military to reposition it for irregular warfare. Its advocates differ in the particulars, but most would expand the Army and Marine Corps; reequip this larger ground force with lighter weapons and vehicles; restructure it to deemphasize traditional armor and artillery in favor of light infantry, civil affairs, military police, military advisor, and special forces capability; and reengineer training, doctrine, Service culture, recruitment, and promotion systems to stress low-intensity irregular warfare skills and methods rather than conventional combat. And major changes in the interagency process would be needed to replace a balkanized, slow-moving decisionmaking system with one agile and integrated enough to compete effectively with politically nimble, media savvy opponents in portraying the results of such warfare persuasively to public audiences overseas. If so, the needed changes in the defense program would be extremely expensive. Many would pay for this by scaling back or abandoning hi-tech air and naval modernization programs; reducing the size of the Air Force and oceangoing Navy; and cutting back the ground forces' training and preparation for conventional war fighting. The result would be a very different American military and defense establishment—from its size to its structure, equipment, people, and doctrine.

Others, however, see Hezbollah's 2006 campaign as a major departure from the asymmetric methods of traditional terrorists or guerrillas and as a shift toward the conventional military methods normally associated with state actors. What is new in this account is how much the 2006 campaign *differed* from terrorist or guerrilla warfare—information age or not—and how conventional and state-like the fighting was. This view of Hezbollah as a conventional army weakens the case for irregular warfare transformation. Instead it implies that a conventionally structured military is actually better suited for a future of nonstate opponents than low-tech transformation advocates claim. Where capabilities for low intensity combat can be improved without undermining conventional performance this would always be wise, but many in this camp see sharp tradeoffs between the forces and training needed for irregular as opposed to conventional combat; if so, then radical transformation would be ill-advised and traditional force structures, doctrines, and training are a better course for the future.

The authors argue in this monograph that neither of these schools' interpretations is completely consistent with Hezbollah's actual conduct of the 2006 campaign, but that the latter is closer than the former. Hezbollah in 2006 used methods very different from those commonly associated with "guerrilla," "terrorist," or "irregular" warfare in important respects: it put too much emphasis on holding ground; it sought concealment chiefly via terrain rather than through civilian intermingling; its forces were too concentrated; and it appears to have articulated a differentiated theater of war for the purpose of defending rocket launch sites to be used in a strategic bombing campaign against Israeli population centers.

But neither did Hezbollah approximate a pure conventional extreme: its defense of ground was too yielding; it relied too extensively on harassing fires and unattended minefields; it put too much emphasis on coercion; and it may have disposed its forces too much in accordance with the population's political orientation, all of which are traits commonly associated with "irregular," or "guerrilla" forces.

Hezbollah's methods were thus somewhere between the popular conceptions of guerrilla and conventional warfare—but so are most military actors', whether state or nonstate. Few real militaries have ever conformed perfectly to either the "conventional" or the "guerrilla" extreme. The commonplace tendency to see guerrilla and conventional methods as a stark dichotomy and to associate the former with nonstate actors and the latter with states is a mistake and has been so for at least a century. In fact, there are profound elements of "guerrilla" methods in the military behavior of almost all state militaries in conventional warfare, from tactics all the way through strategy. And most nonstate guerrilla organizations have long used tactics and strategies that most observers tend to associate with state military behavior. In reality, there is a continuum of methods between the polar extremes of the Maginot Line and the Viet Cong, and most real-world cases have always fallen somewhere in between. The 2006 Lebanon campaign, too, fell somewhere in between. Its placement on this continuum, however, is much further from the Viet Cong end of the scale than many low-tech transformation advocates would expect for a nonstate actor—and, in fact, the biggest divergence between Hezbollah's methods and those of modern Western militaries may well be Hezbollah's imperfect proficiency of execution rather than the doctrine they were trying to execute.

Hezbollah did some things well, such as its use of cover and concealment, its preparation of fighting positions, its fire discipline and mortar marksmanship, and its coordination of direct fire support. But it also fell far short of contemporary Western standards in controlling large-scale maneuver, integrating movement and indirect fire support, combining multiple combat arms, reacting flexibly to changing conditions, and small-arms marksmanship. Hezbollah appears to have *attempted* a remarkably conventional system of tactics and theater operational art, but there is a difference between trying and achieving, and in 2006 at least, Hezbollah's reach in some ways exceeded its grasp.

Yet Hezbollah is hardly alone in this. Many state actors have fallen far short of Western standards of military proficiency, both in today's world and historically. Saddam's "elite" Iraqi state Republican Guard, for example, proved systematically incapable of integrating movement and indirect fire support, combining multiple combat arms, reacting flexibly to changing conditions, or consistently hitting targets with either small *or* large caliber weapons; in two wars with the United States, the Iraqi state military's use of cover and concealment, combat position preparation, and fire discipline were consistently far *less* proficient than Hezbollah's. The Italian state military in 1941 proved much less proficient in conventional warfare than did Hezbollah in 2006; French defenses on the critical Sedan front in 1940 were more exposed, and no more able to react to changing conditions than Hezbollah's. The Egyptian state military proved systematically less adept than Hezbollah in cover and concealment, and little better than Hezbollah in coordinating large scale maneuver with combined arms or flexibly responding to changing conditions in 1956 or 1967; the Syrian state military did no better in 1967, 1973, or 1982. In fact, Hezbollah inflicted more Israeli casualties per Arab fighter in 2006 than did any of Israel's state opponents in the 1956, 1967, 1973, or 1982 Arab-Israeli interstate wars. Hezbollah's skills in conventional warfighting were clearly imperfect in 2006—but they were also well within the observed bounds of other state military actors in the Middle East and elsewhere, and significantly superior to many such states.

In all, then, Hezbollah's behavior in 2006 conformed to neither an ideal model of "guerrilla" warfare nor one of "conventional" warfighting, but its approach and proficiency nonetheless place it well within a band that has characterized many past state militaries in interstate conflicts.

This, however, poses serious challenges for U.S. policymakers in light of the tension between the implications of the 2006 Lebanon campaign and the demands of Iraq and Afghanistan. Ongoing operations in Iraq and Afghanistan demand maximum capability for defeating current enemies who practice a close approximation of classical guerrilla warfare; Lebanon suggests a possibility for future enemies who could wage war more conventionally than this. The different demands of these different styles of fighting thus leave defense planners with a dilemma: the United States cannot simultaneously maximize its potential for both, but neither prospect can safely be ignored, requiring a painful choice in which something important must be sacrificed whichever choice one makes.

By contrast, many in today's future warfare debate see a simpler, less conflicted picture. It is widely argued that the future is one of nonstate opponents who will use asymmetric, irregular methods much like those of today's Iraqi or Afghan insurgents. If so, then there is little or no real, meaningful risk in transforming the U.S. military around the needs of the guerrilla end of the behavioral spectrum. On the contrary, this would unambiguously improve U.S. national security by reshaping the military to meet the real needs of the future, finally shedding the inherited baggage of a Cold War force whose bureaucratic inertia had thwarted needed change until now. If the future really is one of nonstate actors waging an information age version of classical guerrilla warfare, then the defense planning challenge of today and tomorrow is a politically demanding but intellectually straightforward matter of pushing hard enough to get a resistant bureaucracy to do the right thing and accept as much irregular warfare transformation as it can be made to swallow.

The Lebanon experience, however, suggests a future of less clarity and more diversity. Lebanon in 2006 shows us a concrete example of a nonstate actor whose military behavior was far from the classical guerrilla model seen in today's Iraq and Afghanistan. And Hezbollah in 2006 is unlikely to be the last of these—although a careful study of the range of nonstate military behavior is beyond the scope of this monograph, there is reason to believe that similar experience has been observed in recent decades in conflicts such as Chechnya, Slovenia, Bosnia, Croatia, Rwanda, and in actions such as Bai Beche or the Shah-i-Kot valley in Afghanistan in 2001-02. It cannot yet be known how broad this trend may be, what its root causes are, or how far it will go—to answer these questions is a critical research requirement for the defense intellectual community. But Hezbollah does demonstrate, unambiguously, that even today's nonstate actors are not limited to the irregular, guerrilla model military methods so often assumed in the future warfare debate.

And this means that the defense planning challenge is more complex than the current debate often implies. There are real risks both in changing too little *and* in changing too much. And to avert failure in Iraq or Afghanistan may require a real sacrifice in meeting future challenges elsewhere that cannot be avoided by ignoring conventional threats or by insisting on balance. The tradeoffs are real, they are not artificial, and the dilemmas they create cannot be ducked.

This certainly does *not* mean that the United States should return to a preclusive focus on major warfare as it did before 2003—or that a Hezbollah threat should replace the Red Army in the Fulda Gap as the focus for U.S. defense planning. The pre-2003 U.S. military was seriously underinvested in capabilities for countering guerrilla methods of the kind we faced increasingly beginning in 2004. And it would be dangerous and unwise to return to the pre-2003 focus and accept the degree of unpreparedness for guerrilla methods this produced.

Nor does this analysis imply that we should accept failure in Iraq or Afghanistan in order to rebalance the military toward more conventional enemies than we face there. Failure in either Iraq or Afghanistan could have grave consequences for U.S. national interests. *Until these theaters are stabilized—or unless stability becomes infeasible—it will be essential to maximize U.S. performance in these ongoing wars even if this reduces future potential for some as-yet unseen war elsewhere.* The analysis of Lebanon above thus does not presuppose appropriate U.S. policy for Iraq or Afghanistan.

What an analysis of Lebanon can do, however, is to show the limits of some prominent analyses of future warfare and to highlight the true dilemmas associated with defense policy decisionmaking. The future is not simply one of guerrilla-like warfare by nonstate actors. And this means that a thoroughgoing transformation to suit the demands of such warfare has real risks and real dangers as well as benefits. It may still be the right policy to shift the U.S. military's focus toward guerrilla warfare, especially relative to the pre-2003 military's radical avoidance of this problem. It may even be the right policy to make a radical shift toward counterguerrilla proficiency if this is the only way to avoid defeat in such wars. Or it may not: an analysis of Lebanon per se cannot establish how much counterguerrilla capability is enough. But to make this decision requires a sound understanding of the costs—as well as the benefits—of all the options. And a true reoptimization of the military for classical guerrilla warfare would entail real costs in a world where Hezbollah-like enemies may become more common over time. There is no escaping this tradeoff via a simple projection of a monolithic future threat, and one need not necessarily be a bureaucratic obstructionist to worry about nonguerrilla enemies. What Hezbollah in 2006 shows is that in defense planning, as in economics, there is no such thing as a free lunch or an unambiguous, risk-free policy. The real world is one of tradeoffs, and all options have downsides—even the options that look most forward-thinking.

THE 2006 LEBANON CAMPAIGN AND THE FUTURE OF WARFARE: IMPLICATIONS FOR ARMY AND DEFENSE POLICY

Debates over the nature of future warfare drive much of U.S. defense planning, from decisions on force structure to resource allocation, modernization, joint doctrine, transformation, and the use of force. And these debates are powerfully influenced by interpretations of recent combat experience—both our own, and others'. Middle Eastern cases have been especially influential in this way. Initial impressions of the lethality of precision guided antitank weapons in the 1973 October War, for example, gave powerful impetus to one of the most sweeping U.S. doctrinal revisions of the Cold War in the development of the Army's Active Defense concept. Accounts of Israeli effectiveness using new air warfare technology in their 1982 war with Syria proved highly influential in the genesis of the Revolution in Military Affairs thesis in the U.S. defense debate.[1]

1. On the October War and Active Defense, see Paul H. Herbert, *Deciding What Has to Be Done: General William E. DePuy and the 1976 Edition of FM 100-5, Operations,* Ft. Leavenworth, KS: Leavenworth Paper No. 16, 1988, esp. pp. 29-36; Jonathan M. House, *Combined Arms Warfare in the Twentieth Century,* Lawrence, KS: University Press of Kansas, 2001, pp. 239-240. On the 1982 War and the RMA, see, e.g., Rebecca Grant, "The Bekaa Valley War," *Air Force Magazine,* June 2002, pp. 58-62; Thierry Gongora and Harald von Riekhoff, "Sizing Up the Revolution in Military Affairs," in Thierry Gongora and Harald von Riekhoff, eds., *Toward a Revolution in Military Affairs,* Westport, CT: Greenwood, 2000, pp. 1-21 at p. 4; Carl Conetta, Charles Knight, and Lutz Unterseher, *Toward Defensive Restructuring in the Middle East,* Project on Defense Alternatives Research Monograph No. 1, February 1991, section 3.1; Ajay Singh, "Time: The New Dimension in War," *Joint Force Quarterly,* Winter 1995-96, pp. 56-61 at 58, 59.

The 2006 conflict between Israel and Hezbollah in Lebanon could prove comparably influential today. A central issue in today's debate is the role of nonstate opponents in defense planning. It is widely believed that such enemies will be increasingly common in the future, and many now advocate sweeping change in U.S. military posture to prepare for this. As a prominent example of a nonstate actor fighting a Westernized state, Hezbollah's 2006 campaign thus offers a window into a kind of warfare that is increasingly central to U.S. defense planning.

Much has already been written about this campaign, especially in Israel, where the issue of Israeli performance and decisionmaking has both military and partisan political implications.[2] Israel's

2. E.g., Eliyahu Winograd *et al., Final Report,* Tel Aviv: The Inquiry Commission to Examine the Events of the Military Campaign in Lebanon 2006, 2008 [in Hebrew]; Ofer Shelah and Yoav Limor, *Captives in Lebanon,* Tel Aviv: Yedioth Ahronoth, 2007 [in Hebrew]; Amir Rapaport, *Friendly Fire,* Tel Aviv: Ma'ariv, 2007 [in Hebrew]; Amos Harel and Avi Issacharoff, *34 Days: Israel, Hezbollah, and the War in Lebanon,* New York: Palgrave Macmillan, 2008; William M. Arkin, *Divining Victory: Airpower in the 2006 Israel-Hezbollah War,* Maxwell Air Force Base, AL: Air University Press, 2007; Andrew Exum, *Hizballah at War: A Military Assessment,* Washington, DC: Washington Institute for Near East Policy, 2006; David Makovsky and Jeffrey White, *Lessons and Implications of the Israel-Hezbollah War: A Preliminary Assessment,* Washington, DC: Washington Institute for Near East Policy, 2006; Matt M. Matthews, *We Were Caught Unprepared: The 2006 Hezbollah-Israeli War,* Ft. Leavenworth, KS: U.S. Army Combat Studies Institute, 2008; Shlomo Brom and Meir Elan, eds., *The Second Lebanon War: Strategic Perspectives,* Tel Aviv: Institute for National Security Studies, 2007; Reuven Erlich and Yoram Kahati, *Hezbollah as a Case Study of the Battle for Hearts and Minds,* Gelilot: Center for Special Studies/ Intelligence and Terrorism Information Center, 2007; Erlich, *The Use of Lebanese Civilians as Human Shields,* Gelilot: Center for Special Studies/Intelligence and Terrorism Information Center, 2006; Uzi Rubin, *The Rocket Campaign against Israel during the 2006 Lebanon War,* Ramat Gan: Begin-Sadat Center for Strategic Studies, 2007;

conduct of the campaign may also hold important lessons for the United States.[3] But just as important is the question of Hezbollah per se and its methods. How

Avi Kober, "The Israel Defense Forces and the Second Lebanon War: Why the Poor Performance?" *Journal of Strategic Studies*, Vol. 31, No. 1, February 2008, pp. 3-40; Kober, "The Second Lebanon War," Begin-Sadat Center for Strategic Studies, Perspectives Paper No. 22, September 2006; Amir Kulick, "Hizbollah vs. the IDF: The Operational Dimension," *Strategic Assessment*, Vol. 9, No. 3, November 2006; Yoaz Hendel, "Failed Tactical Intelligence in the Lebanon War," *Strategic Assessment*, Vol. 9, No. 3, November 2006; Noam Ophir, "Back to Ground Rules: Some Limitations of Airpower in the Lebanon War," *Strategic Assessment*, Vol. 9, No. 2, August 2006; Efraim Inbar, "Strategic Follies: Israel's Mistakes in the Second Lebanese War," Begin-Sadat Center for Strategic Studies, Perspectives Paper No. 21, September 2006; Alon Ben-David, "Israel Reflects: New Model Army?" *Jane's Defence Weekly*, October 11, 2006; Ben-David, "Debriefing Teams Brand IDF Doctrine 'Completely Wrong'," *Jane's Defence Weekly*, January 3, 2007; Uri Bar-Joseph, "Israel's Military Intelligence Perfomance in the Second Lebanon War," *International Journal of Intelligence and Counter-Intelligence*, Vol. 20, No. 4, January 2007, pp. 583-601; Ralph Peters, "Lessons from Lebanon: The New Model Terrorist Army," *Armed Forces Journal*, Vol. 144, No. 3, October 2006; Anthony H. Cordesman, "The Lessons of the Israeli-Lebanon War: A Briefing" (Washington, DC: Center for Strategic and International Studies, 2008) [accessed on May 1, 2008 at *www.csis.org/media/csis/pubs/080311_lessonleb-iswar.pdf*]; Daniel Byman and Steven Simon, "The No-Win Zone," *The National Interest*, Vol. 86, November/December, 2006, pp. 55-61; Sarah E. Kreps, "The 2006 Lebanon War: Lessons Learned," *Parameters*, Vol. 37, No. 1, Spring 2007, pp. 72-83; Nicholas Blanford, "Deconstructing Hizbullah's Surprise Military Prowess," *Jane's Intelligence Review*, November 1, 2006; Steven Erlanger and Richard A. Oppel, Jr., "A Disciplined Hezbollah Surprises Israel with its Training, Tactics, and Weapons," *New York Times*, August 7, 2006, p. A8; Jonathan D. Zagdanski, "Round 2 in Lebanon," *Infantry*, September/October 2007, pp. 32-35.

3. See, e.g., Matthews, *We Were Caught Unprepared*; Peters, "Lessons from Lebanon"; Exum, *Hizballah at War*, p. 14; Cordesman, "The Lessons of the Israeli-Lebanon War"; Byman and Simon, "The No-Win Zone"; Kreps, "The 2006 Lebanon War," pp. 72-83.

did this nonstate actor wage war in 2006? What were its strengths, weaknesses, tactics, and strategies, and what do these imply for the design of Western militaries that may have to fight similar opponents in the future?

For now, answers to these questions differ. One school sees Hezbollah as an essentially terrorist organization using an information-age version of the asymmetric military methods seen as typical of nonstate actors historically. In this view, Hezbollah's goal was to win an information war for public opinion within and beyond Lebanon, solidifying its political position as the standard-bearer for Arab resistance to Israel by drawing Israel into a guerrilla war it could not win while publicizing the inevitable Israeli miscues and civilian fatalities. The tactics to implement this strategy are seen as a higher-tech version of standard guerrilla warfare: sniping, albeit with modern antitank missiles; hit-and-run ambushes; roadside bombs; harassing mortar and rocket fire, often against civilian targets in Israel; the use of Lebanese civilians as human shields to protect guerrillas against Israeli firepower; and efforts to goad a state military into over-use of violence and widespread killings of innocents. What was new, in this account, was mainly Hezbollah's use of the internet and sympathetic cable news networks to publicize its military actions, which are held to have been intended chiefly as spectacles to attract this publicity.[4]

---

4. See, e.g., Gabriel Siboni, "The Military Campaign in Lebanon," in Brom and Elan, *The Second Lebanon War*, pp. 62-63; Erlich and Kahati, *Hezbollah as a Case Study of the Battle for Hearts and Minds*; Erlich, *The Use of Lebanese Civilians as Human Shields*; Kreps, "The 2006 Lebanon War"; Edward Cody and Molly Moore, "The Best Guerrilla Force in the World," *Washington Post*, August 14 2006, p. A01; Kober, "The Second Lebanon War," p. 2.

Others, however, see Hezbollah's 2006 campaign as a major departure from the asymmetric methods of traditional terrorists or guerrillas and as a shift toward the conventional military methods normally associated with state actors. In this view, Hezbollah is said to have defended ground, to have prepared positions for sustained combat in defense of that ground, and to have maneuvered conventionally armed, trained, and equipped combatants in an attempt to defeat an Israeli invasion in a way that resembled traditional state military doctrines more closely than a traditional terrorist organization could. What was new, in this alternative account, is how much the 2006 campaign *differed* from terrorist or guerrilla warfare—information age or not—and how conventional and state-like the fighting was.[5]

These contrasting views imply very different policy agendas for the United States. An account of Hezbollah as an information-age guerrilla force strengthens the case for a major redesign of the U.S. military to reposition it for irregular warfare. For over a decade, critics have argued that the United States is over-invested in conventional capability and should restructure for irregular or low intensity conflict; the guerrilla war in Iraq has turned this argument into something approaching conventional wisdom in the U.S. debate today. An interpretation of the 2006 campaign as irregular warfare reinforces the associated case for what might be termed the "low-tech transformation" agenda. Its advocates differ in the particulars, but most would expand the Army and Marine Corps; reequip this larger ground force

5. See, e.g., Exum, *Hizballah at War*; Erlanger and Oppel, "A Disciplined Hezbollah Surprises Israel with its Training, Tactics, and Weapons," p. A8; Zagdanski, "Round 2 in Lebanon," pp. 32-35.

with lighter weapons and vehicles; restructure it to deemphasize traditional armor and artillery in favor of light infantry, civil affairs, military police, military advisor, and special forces capability; and reengineer training, doctrine, Service culture, recruitment, and promotion systems to stress low-intensity irregular warfare skills and methods rather than conventional combat. And major changes in the interagency process would be needed to replace a balkanized, slow-moving decisionmaking system with one agile and integrated enough to compete effectively with politically nimble, media savvy opponents in portraying the results of such warfare persuasively to public audiences overseas. If so, the needed changes in the defense program would be extremely expensive; many would pay for this by scaling back or abandoning hi-tech air and naval modernization programs; reducing the size of the Air Force and oceangoing Navy; and cutting back the ground forces' training and preparation for conventional war fighting. The result would be a very different American military and defense establishment—from its size to its structure, equipment, people, and doctrine.[6]

---

6. See, e.g., Thomas X. Hammes, *The Sling and the Stone: On War in the 21st Century*, St. Paul, MN: Zenith Press, 2004. For related arguments, see Frederick Kagan, *Finding the Target: The Transformation of American Military Policy*, New York: Encounter Books, 2006; Max Boot, "The Struggle to Transform the Military," *Foreign Affairs*, Vol. 84, No. 2, March/April 2005, pp. 103-118; Niall Ferguson, *Colossus: The Price of America's Empire*, New York: Penguin, 2004; Robert Kaplan, *Imperial Grunts: The American Military on the Ground*, New York: Random House, 2005; Hans Binnendijk and Stuart E. Johnson, eds., *Transforming for Stability and Reconstruction Operations*, Washington, DC: National Defense University Press, 2004; John A. Nagl, *Institutionalizing Adaptation: It's Time for a Permanent Army Advisory Corps*, Washington, DC: Center for a New American Security, 2007; Tom Donnelly, "The Army We Need," *The Weekly Standard*, June 4, 2007; Charles Barry, "Organizing Land Forces for Stability Operations," National

Conversely, an account of Hezbollah as a conventional army weakens the case for such transformation. Instead it implies that a conventionally structured military is actually better suited for a future of nonstate opponents than low-tech transformation advocates claim. Where capabilities for low-intensity combat can be improved without undermining conventional performance this would always be wise, but many in this camp see sharp tradeoffs between the forces and training needed for irregular as opposed to conventional combat; if so, then radical transformation would be ill-advised and traditional force structures, doctrines, and training are a better course for the future.[7]

We will argue below that neither of these schools' interpretations is completely consistent with Hezbollah's actual conduct of the 2006 campaign, but that the latter is closer than the former. That is, Hezbollah's methods were somewhere between the popular conceptions of guerrilla and conventional warfare—but so are most military actors, whether state or nonstate. The commonplace tendency to see guerrilla and conventional methods as a stark dichotomy is a

---

Defense University and National Security Policy Short Course on Force Structure for Stability Operations and Interagency Integration, 2007; David Betz, "Redesigning Land Forces for Wars Among the People," *Contemporary Security Policy*, Vol. 28, No. 2, August 2007, pp. 221-243; Robert M. Perito, *Where is the Lone Ranger When We Need Him? America's Search for a Post-Conflict Stability Force*, Washington, DC: United States Institute of Peace, 2004.

7. See, e.g., Matthews, *We Were Caught Unprepared*; Gian P. Gentile, "Misreading the Surge Threatens U.S. Army's Conventional Capabilities," *World Politics Review*, March 4, 2008; Sean McFarland, Michael Shields, and Jeffrey Snow, "The King and I: The Impending Crisis in Field Artillery's Ability to Provide Fire Support to Maneuver Commanders," White Paper for U.S. Army Chief of Staff, nd.

mistake and has been so for at least a century. In fact, there are profound elements of "guerrilla" methods in the military behavior of almost all state militaries in conventional warfare, from tactics all the way through strategy. And most nonstate guerrilla organizations have long used tactics and strategies that most observers tend to associate with state military behavior. In reality, there is a continuum of methods between the polar extremes of the Maginot Line and the Viet Cong, and most real-world cases fall somewhere in between. The 2006 Lebanon campaign, too, fell somewhere in between. Its placement on this continuum, however, is much further from the Viet Cong end of the scale than many low-tech transformation advocates assume—and, in fact, the biggest divergence between Hezbollah's methods and those of modern Western militaries may well be Hezbollah's imperfect proficiency of execution rather than the doctrine they were trying to execute.

We base this assessment chiefly on a series of 36 primary-source interviews with Israeli participants in the campaign who were in a position to observe Hezbollah's actual behavior in the field in 2006, coupled with deductive inference from observable Hezbollah behavior in the field to findings for their larger strategic intent for the campaign.[8] Where possible, we supplement this with evidence drawn

8. Interviewees range in rank from Brigadier General to Second Lieutenant, and included commanders at company, battalion, or brigade level from a majority of Israeli brigades engaged, and from all major sectors of the campaign. Audiotapes documenting these interviews have been deposited at the U.S. Army Military History Institute (MHI) archive in Carlisle, Pennsylvania, and include full identifying information for all interviewees. At the request of the Israel Defense Force, the full identification of interviewees is held at MHI as Official Use Only; documentation below uses rank and first initial only, but this information is sufficient to enable all cited information to be confirmed by those with appropriate clearance.

from Israeli interviews with a handful of captured Hezbollah fighters, but we had no systematic access to the Hezbollah side in the war, hence our findings are drawn from a combination of Israeli observational evidence and deduction from this.

We present the resulting analysis in six steps. First we develop a taxonomy of military behavior, treating this as a continuum rather than a dichotomy of "irregular" and "conventional," and arguing that most real cases fall somewhere in the middle of the theoretical range. Second, we outline the key events of the campaign. We then characterize Hezbollah's tactics in 2006 by reference to the taxonomy. Next, we do the same for their strategy and theater operations. We follow this with an assessment of Hezbollah's proficiency in executing these methods. We conclude with a summary assessment and implications for U.S. Army and Defense policy.

TAXONOMY

"Irregular," guerrilla, or "asymmetric" warfare has usually been treated as a sharp dichotomy with conventional or "combined arms" warfare in the U.S. debate. And clearly there are major differences between the military methods of Sunni insurgents in Iraq and Saddam's Republican Guard, for example. But there are also a number of important similarities. Many of the differences, moreover, are variations of degree rather than kind, and even differences of kind do not readily sort themselves into a handful of neat, categorical alternatives.

An intention to hold ground, for example, is commonly associated with conventional warfare. Guerrillas, by contrast, are typically assumed to favor hit-and-run methods in which retention of ground is not attempted and in which the guerrillas' orientation is to the enemy, not the terrain per se. That is, the classical guerrilla chooses terrain based solely on its potential to enable casualty infliction on the enemy, not for its control. Guerrillas are expected to melt away when attacked by superior government forces rather than to stand their ground and accept decisive engagement, and they often prefer booby traps, mines, roadside bombs, or harassing rocket or mortar fire meant to inflict casualties without denying the opponent access to an area per se.[9]

---

9. "Decisive engagement" is a condition wherein defenders remain in position under assault even after the attackers have gotten close enough that the defenders cannot readily withdraw without being overrun. As the Defense Department defines it: "In land and naval warfare, an engagement in which a unit is considered fully committed and cannot maneuver or extricate itself. In the absence of outside assistance, the action must be fought to a conclusion and either won or lost with the forces at hand." [*www.js.pentagon.mil/doctrine/jel/doddict/data/d/01536.html*] On the unwillingness of classical guerrillas to accept decisive engagement for the defense of ground, see, e.g., Mao Tse-Tung, *On Guerrilla Warfare,* Samuel B. Griffith, trans., Mineola, NY: Dover, 2005, pp. 52, 97, 102; Ernesto Guevara, *Guerrilla Warfare,* Old Chelsea, NY: Ocean Press, 2006, pp. 20, 22, 26; Ian F.W. Beckett, *Modern Insurgencies and Counter-Insurgencies,* New York: Routledge, 2001, p. 2; Bard E. O'Neill, *Insurgency & Terrorism: Inside Modern Revolutionary Warfare,* Dulles, VA: Brassey's, 1990, pp. 25-26; Anthony James Joes, *Resisting Rebellion: The History and Politics of Counterinsurgency,* Lexington, KY: University Press of Kentucky, 2004, p. 18; Walter Laqueur, *Guerrilla: A Historical and Critical Study,* Boston: Little, Brown, 1976, pp. viii, 3; Robert B. Asprey, *War in the Shadows: The Guerrilla in History,* vol. 1, Garden City, NY: Doubleday, 1975, p. xi; Steven Metz and Raymond Millen, *Insurgency and Counterinsurgency in the 21st Century: Reconceptualizing Threat and Response,* Carlisle, PA: U.S. Army War College Strategic Studies Institute, 2004, p. 2; Harel and Issacharoff, *34 Days,* p. 129.

All of these techniques, however, are standard elements of orthodox conventional doctrine, too. Delaying actions, for example, are a normal element of any theater defense. In a delaying action, defenders trade space for time, weakening the attacker as it advances, disrupting the attacker's formations and, if possible, demoralizing its troops—but without accepting decisive engagement and without expecting to retain any particular piece of ground.[10] Mobile defense, one of the three basic forms of defensive maneuver in orthodox conventional doctrine, orients the defender on the enemy's forces rather than on particular terrain; terrain is chosen to facilitate the destruction of the enemy, which is the primary objective. Mobile defenses normally involve delaying actions along the attacker's axis of advance; delays without decisive engagement are also central to the conduct of conventional covering force operations in the forward sectors of prepared defenses in depth.[11] Ambush, moreover, is a standard technique in orthodox defense, in which defenders strive to remain hidden and undetected until attackers have entered a designated kill sack where they can be surprised and taken under sudden and concentrated fire. Such defenders may or may not hold their positions until decisively engaged.[12] Harassing fires from mortars or artillery are common means by which conventional defenders seek to disrupt or interdict enemy movement in otherwise apparently safe rear

---

10. See, e.g., *FM 3.0: Operations*, Washington, DC: Headquarters, Department of the Army, 2001, paras. 8-28 through 8-31; *FM 71-1, Tank and Mechanized Infantry Company Team*, Washington, DC: Headquarters, Department of the Army, 1998, ch. 4, section 6.

11. See, e.g., *FM 3.0: Operations*, paras. 8-14 through 8-19.

12. See, e.g., *FM 71-1, Tank and Mechanized Infantry Company Team*, ch. 3, Section 6; ch. 4.

areas; mines are sometimes used to defend ground that must be retained, but are also used elsewhere to delay, disrupt, or inflict casualties on attackers in transit without denying them access directly.[13] Orthodox conventional defense thus commonly includes many actions which do not hold ground per se or accept decisive engagement.

Of course, there are normally geographical limits to delay and harassment in conventional defense; conventional defenders will not allow an invader access to the entire national territory without making a stand somewhere. Ultimately, a conventional defense is intended to leave the defender in control of the country. But even guerrillas often have limits on their willingness to allow an enemy to move: critical locations such as base camps or weapon caches can sometimes be defended by fighters who accept decisive engagement in such locations.[14] And many guerrilla

13. See, e.g., *FM 5-102, Countermobility,* Washington, DC: Headquarters, Department of the Army, 1985, ch. 2; *FM 6-20-30, Tactics, Techniques, and Procedures for Fire Support for Corps and Division Operations*, Washington, DC: Headquarters, Department of the Army, 1989, appendix B, sections I and II.

14. During the Chinese civil war from 1945-49, for instance, communist forces attempted to hold several cities in the face of nationalist offensives: in 1945, 110,000 communist troops suffered 40,000 casualties in a failed defense of Szeping; in 1946, 20,000 of 70,000 communists were killed trying to defend Jukao; in 1947, 20,000 of 60,000 communists were killed when nationalist forces relieved the siege of Tehwei. (Figures from Micheal Clodfelter, *Warfare and Armed Conflicts: A Statistical Reference to Casualty and Other Figures, 1500-2000,* 2nd ed., Jefferson, NC: McFarland, 2002, pp. 695-696.) Greek insurgents concentrated 12,000 fighters in the Grammos Mountain region in 1949; they suffered large numbers of casualties attempting to protect the area, and could no longer continue significant resistance. (Joes, *Resisting Rebellion,* pp. 185-186) FARC guerrillas in Colombia have demonstrated the willingness and capability to resist combined ground-air attacks from government forces (David Spencer, "Bogota Continues to Bleed as FARC Find their Military Feet," *Jane's Intelligence Review,*

wars are fought over political control of a country—as with conventional defense, the ultimate aim of many guerrilla forces is to establish political control over a geographically contiguous polity.[15]

Concealment is another trait often held to distinguish conventional from guerrilla warfare. Concealment is typically seen as critical for guerrilla forces, which depend on this for survival in the face of superior government militaries.[16] Yet even in conventional warfare, exposure frequently means death. The modern battlefield is so lethal that it has been suicidal to allow massed formations to be caught exposed in the open since at least 1914. In fact, concealment—and the techniques needed to provide it as technology has changed—has arguably been the single most important theme in the history of modern conventional tactics.[17] A distinguishing feature of post-1914 conventional warfare has been the "empty battlefield" that resulted from the widespread adoption of cover and concealment in modern high-intensity combat; soldiers in such wars commonly develop an instinctive suspicion of conditions that "seem too quiet" precisely because conventional defenders are commonly invisible to attackers much of

---

November 1, 1998; Jeremy McDermott, "Colombian Insurgency Escalates as Guerrillas Go Back on Offensive," *Jane's Intelligence Review*, July 1, 2005). Guerrilla groups have conducted numerous offensives and sieges against important strategic locations: prominent examples include the 1968 Tet Offensive in Vietnam, the 1975 Khmer Rouge offensive against Phnom Penh, the 1989 FMLN offensive against San Salvador, and the Chinese communist attack on Suchow in 1948 (See, e.g., Clodfelter, *Warfare and Armed Conflicts*, pp. 689-690, 696, 712, 757-759).

15. See, e.g., Mao, *On Guerrilla Warfare*, pp. 55-57, 113; Beckett, *Modern Insurgencies and Counter-Insurgencies*, pp. 75-76.

16. See, e.g., Mao, *On Guerrilla Warfare*, p. 97; Guevara, *Guerrilla Warfare*, p. 22; O'Neill, *Insurgency & Terrorism*, pp. 53-57.

17. For a more detailed discussion, see Stephen Biddle, *Military Power: Explaining Victory and Defeat in Modern Battle*, Princeton:

the time.[18] Of course, there are differences in the *way* conventional armies and guerrilla forces obtain the needed concealment—although both use the natural complexity of the terrain to conceal themselves (indeed guerrillas classically exploit mountains, jungles, or other unusually complex terrain for this purpose), guerrillas also typically try to conceal themselves via intermingling with an indistinguishable civilian population. Classical guerrilla tactics assume either that the government will be loathe to harm apparently innocent civilians, or that the government will suffer politically from doing so. Hence many guerrillas wear civilian clothing and live, train, and fight among civilian populations as a means of rendering themselves as difficult as possible to distinguish from those civilians.[19] Conventional armies, by contrast, wear distinguishing uniforms, occupy distinct bases, and often fight in rural areas away from civilian population centers. But even here, the difference is often less clear than it seems. Urban warfare has long been a major feature of even conventional warfare (Stalingrad, Berlin, Caen, and Aachen were among the many cities destroyed by ground combat in World War II); villages and other built-up areas are traditionally exploited as favorable

Princeton University Press, 2004, chs. 3 and 4.

18. See, e.g., Richard Holmes, *Acts of War: The Behavior of Men in Battle*, New York: Free Press, 1986; Christopher Hamner, "Enduring Danger, Surviving Fear: Combat Experience and American Infantrymen in the War for Independence, the Civil War, and the Second World War," Ph.D. dissertation, Department of History, University of North Carolina, 2004, e.g., pp. 11, 29, 36, 54, 109, 141, 185-186, 198-199.

19. See, e.g., Mao, *On Guerrilla Warfare*, pp. 92-93; Guevara, *Guerrilla Warfare*, pp. 19-20, 26; Rupert Smith, *The Utility of Force: The Art of War in the Modern World*, New York: Alfred A. Knopf, 2007, pp. 280-286; Beckett, *Modern Insurgencies and Counter-Insurgencies*, p. 2; Joes, *Resisting Rebellion*, p. 13; Richard Clutterbuck, *Guerrillas and Terrorists*, Athens, OH: Ohio University Press, 1980, p. 26; David Kilcullen, "Counterinsurgency Redux," *Survival*, Vol. 48, No. 4, December 2006, p. 119.

defensive ground in conventional warfare precisely because of the superior concealment and cover they offer; civilians are often killed in greater number than uniformed soldiers in conventional combat because even the use of uniforms does not always enable combatants to distinguish or discriminate from a distance or in the heat of battle; and all of this is becoming increasingly characteristic of conventional warfare as cities grow and economies urbanize around the world.[20] Concealment is thus critical in all modern warfare, guerrilla or conventional, and the difference between an emphasis on terrain for such purposes in conventional warfare and civilian intermingling in guerrilla warfare is more a difference in emphasis and relative incidence than a sharp distinction of kind.

Dispersion and the apparent absence of distinctions between a contested front and a safe rear area are other traits commonly associated with guerrilla warfare. Guerrillas are normally assumed to avoid concentration and instead to spread themselves over large areas in small, independent formations, using stealth, concealment, and infiltration to afford them access to any part of a theater and often choosing preferentially to attack "soft" logistical or support targets in nominal rear areas.[21] Yet dispersion, like

20. On urban combat in conventional warfare, see Michael C. Desch, ed., *Soldiers in Cities: Military Operations on Urban Terrain*, Carlisle, PA: Strategic Studies Institute, U.S. Army War College, 2001; William G. Robertson and Lawrence A. Yates, eds., *Block by Block: The Challenges of Urban Operations*, Ft. Leavenworth, KS: U.S. Army Command and General Staff College Press, 2003; *FM 90-10: Military Operations on Urban Terrain*, Washington, DC: Headquarters, U.S. Department of the Army, 1979; *Handbook for Joint Urban Operations*, Washington, DC: The Joint Staff, 2000; John A. English, *On Infantry*, New York: Praeger, 1984, pp. 185-216.

21. See, e.g., Mao, *On Guerrilla Warfare*, pp. 52, 97-98, 102-104; O'Neill, *Insurgency & Terrorism*, pp. 25-26, 37; Joes, *Resisting Rebellion*, pp. 12-13, 19; Laqueur, *Guerrilla*, pp. viii, 124-125; Asprey, *War in the Shadows*, p. xi; Kilcullen, "Counterinsurgency

concealment, has been a central theme in the history of modern conventional tactics. As early as 1917, conventional militaries discovered that they could not exploit the potential cover inherent in rural terrain while operating in large, concentrated formations. The natural complexity of the earth's surface provides an enormous amount of potential cover from enemy fire, but such "dead ground" is irregularly distributed and often broken into tiny patches. To take advantage of this potential, massed linear formations had to be broken down into small groups with only handfuls of soldiers, sprinting from cover to cover on the basis of the vagaries of the ground rather than the progress of their neighbors. Movement in the presence of the enemy came to depend increasingly on working small groups forward unobserved, using a combination of concealment and suppressive fire to keep them from being annihilated by enemy fire en route. The resulting techniques have sometimes been called "infiltration tactics" as a result, and infiltration per se, often at night, is a standard movement method for infantry in orthodox conventional armies.[22] Coupled with the increas-

---

Redux," pp. 117-118, 120; Metz and Millen, *Insurgency and Counterinsurgency*, p. 6.

22. See, e.g., *FM 71-1, Tank and Mechanized Infantry Company Team*, Washington, DC: Headquarters, Department of the Army, 1998, ch. 3, Section 2; on "infiltration tactics" in World War I, see, e.g., Timothy Lupfer, *The Dynamics of Doctrine: Changes in German Tactical Doctrine During the First World War*, Ft. Leavenworth, KS: U.S. Army Combat Studies Institute, 1981, Leavenworth Paper No.4, pp. 43-46; Shelford Bidwell and Dominick Graham, *Firepower: British Army Weapons and Theories of War, 1904-1945*, London: Allen and Unwin, 1985, pp. 94-130, 139-146; Paddy Griffith, *Battle Tactics of the Western Front*, New Haven: Yale University Press, 1994, pp. 93-100, 120-158; Bruce Gudmundsson, *Stormtroop Tactics: Innovation in the German Army, 1914-1918*, New York: Praeger, 1989; English, *On Infantry*, pp. 17-26; J.B.A. Bailey, *Field Artillery and Firepower*, Oxford: Military Press, 1989, pp. 141-152; Robin Prior and Trevor Wilson, *Command on the Western*

ing depth of modern defenses—the Soviet defensive system at Kursk in 1943, for example, extended over a distance of more than 100 miles from the front line[23]—this dispersion has often resulted in deliberately porous defensive systems in which individual positions have had to be prepared for 360-degree defense and in which friendly and hostile forces are often intermingled in ways that blur the distinction between front and rear. The increasing reach of standoff fires, moreover, has extended the threat of attack even further away from the nominal front. For Germans on the Western Front in 1944, for example, no location was truly safe from Allied air attack: German General Erwin Rommel was famously wounded during an administrative movement in a nominal rear area in France during the Normandy campaign when his staff car was strafed by an Allied fighter; in today's era of deep strike by precision air or missile forces, even the conventional battlefield has much less guarantee of safety in the rear than it once did.[24]

Contrasts in strategic intent are another distinction often drawn between guerrilla and conventional warfare. In particular, conventional strategy is often seen as an exercise in what Thomas Schelling termed *brute force*; guerrilla strategy is usually seen as *coercive* (and sometimes *persuasive*). Coercive strategies work by convincing the enemy to give you what you want by threatening pain if they do not (persuasion strategies induce a similar decision via positive inducement rather than negative sanction). Brute force strategies

Front, Oxford: Blackwell, 1992, pp. 311-315, 362-366; G.C. Wynne, *If Germany Attacks: The Battle in Depth in the West*, London: Faber and Faber, Ltd., 1940; Greenwood Press reprint, 1976, p. 327.

23. Jeffrey Jukes, *Kursk, The Clash of Armor*, New York: Ballantine, 1968, p. 54.

24. Max Hastings, *Overlord*, New York: Simon and Schuster, 1984, p. 176.

work by taking what you want through force without requiring any meaningful decision on the enemy's part.[25] Guerrillas, in the typical view, are too weak to prevail by brute force destruction of the enemy outright, hence they must resort to manipulating others' decision calculus via some combination of persuasion and coercive pain infliction as their only real options—they aim either to convince civilians to oppose the state, or to kill enough state soldiers or destroy enough state value for the government (or its foreign backers) to decide that the cost exceeds the stake at issue in the war, yielding political concession to guerrilla demands. States engaged in conventional warfare, by contrast, are thought to have the material resources to pursue their aims by brute force and to prefer this. The very term "asymmetric warfare" stems from this perceived distinction: traditional interstate warfare is "symmetric" because both sides are strong enough to use brute force methods against the other; wars between state and nonstate actors are "asymmetric" because the state is assumed to adopt conventional brute force whereas its weaker nonstate enemy chooses a different, coercive, approach instead.[26]

---

25. Thomas Schelling, *Arms and Influence*, New Haven: Yale University Press, 1966, pp. 2-6ff.

26. See, e.g., Ivan Arreguin-Toft, *How the Weak Win Wars: A Theory of Asymmetric Conflict*, Cambridge: Cambridge University Press, 2005; Hammes, *The Sling and the Stone*; Roger W. Barnett, *Asymmetrical Warfare: Today's Challenge to U.S. Military Power*, Washington, DC: Brassey's, 2003; H. John Poole, *Tactics of the Crescent Moon: Militant Muslim Combat Methods*, Emerald Isle, NC: Posterity Press, 2004; Smith, *The Utility of Force*; Frank Kitson, *Low Intensity Operations: Subversion, Insurgency, Peace-Keeping*, Harrisburg, PA: Stackpole, 1971; Gil Merom, *How Democracies Lose Small Wars: State, Society, and the Failures of France in Algeria, Israel, and Lebanon, and the United States in Vietnam*, New York: Cambridge University Press, 2003; O'Neill, *Insurgency & Terrorism*; Joes, *Resisting*

Yet most states use coercive strategies, too, either alone or in conjunction with brute force. Allied strategy in World War II, for example, involved a great deal of brute force—the intended destruction of Axis militaries—but it also embraced a strategic bombing campaign whose intent was largely coercive. That is, the Allies hoped that the destruction of hostile economic assets and population centers would impose so much pain on enemy societies as to convince their leaders to make peace in order to halt the bombing. Many Allied leaders hoped that this could be accomplished without brute force land invasions of Germany or Japan, and in fact Japan surrendered before the home islands were conquered.[27] American strategy in 1991 was a mix of brute force in the ground war to drive Saddam out of Kuwait, and coercion in a strategic bombing campaign intended to increase Saddam's costs by

---

Rebellion; Richard H. Shultz and Andrea J. Dew, *Insurgents, Terrorists, and Militias: The Warriors of Contemporary Combat,* New York: Columbia University Press, 2006, pp. 18-54; Metz and Millen, *Insurgency and Counterinsurgency,* pp. 2, 6; Andrew J. R. Mack, "Why Big Nations Lose Small Wars: The Politics of Asymmetric Conflict," *World Politics,* Vol. 27, No. 2, January, 1975, pp. 175-200; Stephen P. Rosen, "War and the Willingness to Suffer," in Bruce M. Russett, ed., *Peace, War and Numbers,* Beverly Hills, CA: Sage, 1972, pp. 167-183.

27. Charles Webster and Noble Frankland, *The Strategic Air Offensive against Germany, 1939-1945,* London: HMSO, 1961; Tami Davis Biddle, *Rhetoric and Reality in Air Warfare: The Evolution of British and American Ideas about Strategic Bombing, 1914-1945,* Princeton: Princeton University Press, 2002, pp. 214-288; Robert A. Pape, *Bombing to Win: Air Power and Coercion in War,* Ithaca, NY: Cornell University Press, 1996, pp. 87-136, 254-313.

destroying valued assets within Iraq until and unless he agreed to withdraw.[28] NATO strategy in 1999 was chiefly coercive, with the primary aim being to impose financial and political pain on Slobodon Milosevic by bombing valued economic assets in Serbia until and unless he halted ethnic cleansing in Kosovo.[29]

Nor is strategic bombing the only form of coercion in conventional interstate warfare. In almost all such wars, the weaker power must ultimately rely on a coercive logic to prevail. In World War II, for example, Japan realized it had no chance of destroying the U.S. military—American population, wealth, and industrial advantages were too great, enabling America to crush Japan militarily if it chose to mobilize fully and pay the price. Japan's only hope was to raise the price of doing so to one that Americans would not pay: by killing enough U.S. soldiers, sailors, and Marines in a tenacious defense of their Pacific conquests, the Japanese hoped to convince the Americans to accept a negotiated peace that would preserve Japanese expansion rather than fighting on until Japan was destroyed.[30] Germany is among the states most often cited as relying on brute force battlefield annihilation

---

28. On the coercive nature of the Gulf War air campaign, see Eliot A. Cohen, Director, *Gulf War Airpower Survey,* Vol. I, Part I: *Planning,* Washington, DC: U.S. Government Printing Office, 1993, pp. 123, 130-131, 163; Pape, *Bombing to Win,* pp. 214-219ff.

29. See, e.g., Ivo H. Daalder and Michael E. O'Hanlon, *Winning Ugly: NATO's War to Save Kosovo,* Washington, DC: Brookings Institution Press, 2000, esp. pp. 91-96, 101, 208-210.

30. James B. Wood, *Japanese Military Strategy in the Pacific War,* Lanham, MD: Rowman & Littlefield, 2007, p. 23; Gerhard L. Weinberg, *A World at Arms: A Global History of World War II,* New York: Cambridge University Press, 1994, pp. 190-191; Woodburn Kirby, *The War against Japan,* Vol. 5, London: HMSO, 1969, pp. 96, 149, 393-406; Robert J. C. Butow, *Japan's Decision to Surrender,* Stanford, CA: Stanford University Press, 1954, p. 43, reference 1; Pape, *Bombing to Win,* pp. 110-113.

of military opponents rather than political coercion.[31] Yet German strategy in both World Wars came to rely increasingly on political coercion rather than military brute force once the tide of battle turned against them. By 1917, for example, no rational German could conclude that an Allied coalition including the distant United States could be militarily destroyed; the only option was to raise the cost of continuing the war to the point where at least some key opponents would accept a negotiated settlement tolerable to Germany, and German strategy increasingly reflected this.[32] In World War II, even Hitler no longer hoped to destroy Allied armies outright or to deny them access to German soil by 1944; instead German strategy hoped to exploit Western war weariness by inflicting casualties, using a form of coercive cost imposition to split the Allied coalition and persuade Western governments to accept a separate peace that would leave Hitler in power.[33] In all three examples—Imperial Japan, Wilhelmine Germany, and Nazi Germany—state governments in "conventional" world wars pursued strategic logics that were centrally coercive. In fact, this is such a

31. See, e.g., Gunther Rothenberg, "Moltke, Schlieffen, and the Problem of Strategic Envelopment," in Peter Paret, ed., *Makers of Modern Strategy*, Princeton: Princeton University Press, 1986, pp. 296-325; Jehuda Wallach, *The Dogma of the Battle of Annihilation*, Westport, CT: Greenwood, 1986; J. P. Harris, "The Myth of Blitzkrieg," *War in History*, Vol. 2, No. 3, November 1995, pp. 335-352.

32. Erich von Falkenhayn, *General Headquarters and Its Critical Decisions*, London: Hutchinson, 1919, p. 216; Ottokar Czernin, *In the World War*, New York: Cassell, 1919, p. 116; Hein Goemans, *War & Punishment: The Causes of War Termination & the First World War*, Princeton: Princeton University Press, 2000, pp. 88, 97.

33. Weinberg, *A World at Arms*, pp. 587-588; John Keegan, *The Second World War*, New York: Penguin, 1990, pp. 209-210; B. H. Liddell Hart, *History of the Second World War*, New York: Putnam's, 1970, pp. 169, 485, 493; Pape, *Bombing to Win*, pp. 288-289.

common great power strategy in major conventional warfare that Clausewitz treats it as a fundamental feature of war per se and discusses it as such explicitly and at length in *On War*.[34]

The ubiquity of coercive strategy in conventional warfare between states creates conceptual problems for the entire notion of "asymmetric" warfare as a rigorous logical distinction. Strictly speaking, almost *all* wars, even conventional, interstate world wars, are asymmetric: the two sides almost never pursue identical strategies, or even broadly similar ones—this would be foolhardy for the weaker contestant. The stronger side often tries to secure its aims by brute force, but the weaker normally adopts some form of coercion. This is hardly unique to guerrilla wars or to conflicts between state and nonstate opponents; a strategic logic based on political coercion does not uniquely distinguish guerrilla from conventional warfare. Of course, there are many varieties of brute force and coercion, and some combatants employ versions of coercion that are superficially more similar to versions of brute force than others; the Viet Cong in 1965 and Sunni insurgents in 2004 obviously fought differently than the Imperial Japanese Army in 1944 or the Iraqi Republican Guard in 1991. But all four of these examples were pursuing strategies of political coercion against opponents that many have characterized as pursuing strategies of conventional military brute force—the actors' strategic logic does not cleanly distinguish "guerrilla" from "conventional," and "asymmetry" is properly regarded as a feature of almost all strategy rather than as a meaningful

34. Carl von Clausewitz, *On War*, Michael Howard and Peter Paret, eds. and trans., Princeton, NJ: Princeton University Press, 1976, pp. 90-99.

distinction between irregular and "regular" warfare.

None of this is to suggest that guerrilla warfare and conventional combat are identical or that there are no important differences. They are obviously not the same thing.

But it is to argue that *the key distinctions are differences of degree not kind.* And this suggests that the difference between "guerrilla" and "conventional" war making is not well-treated as a dichotomy, but is more accurately described as a continuum.

Figure 1 presents this continuum in graphical form. At one extreme would be historical cases such as the French defense of the Maginot Line in 1940. Such cases involve tactical dispositions where combatants are expected to fight mostly from static, prepared positions with a minimum of movement; decisive engagement is routinely accepted, and little ground is to be yielded voluntarily; dispositions are oriented much more to the terrain and much less to the enemy's particular locations; dispositions are relatively concentrated with a large fraction of the total deployed forward near the international border or the current frontier dividing clear spheres of control; and concealment is obtained by use of the terrain, often augmented by elaborate man-made camouflage or terrain modification. Strategy in this extreme would involve an emphasis on brute force prevention of enemy entry into friendly territory or brute force destruction of enemy forces outright.

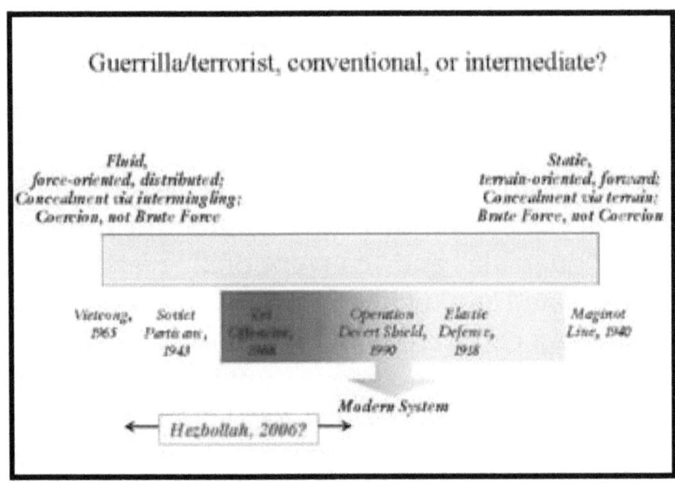

Figure 1. A Taxonomy of Military Behavior.

At the opposite extreme would be historical cases such as the Viet Cong in 1965. Such cases involve tactical dispositions where combatants rarely fight from static, prepared positions or accept decisive engagement; combat normally involves movement; ground is rarely contested per se; dispositions and maneuver are oriented much more to the enemy rather than the terrain; dispositions are widely dispersed over large areas with little apparent orientation to any geographic border and no apparent distinction between front and rear; and concealment is obtained chiefly by intermingling with an indistinguishable civilian population. Strategy in this extreme would emphasize political coercion via the infliction of casualties and other costs, rather than brute force destruction of the enemy outright or any absolute ability to deny the enemy access to friendly territory.

These two extremes represent the closest cases to "pure" guerrilla or conventional war fighting styles.

Very few real-world cases conform perfectly to either extreme, however; almost all fall somewhere in between.

The German "elastic defense" on the Western Front from 1916-18, for example, obtained concealment via the terrain and disposed its forces largely around the nature of the terrain rather than the enemy's locations, but it was distributed over a depth of 3 to 10 miles, and was built around the assumption that ground would not be held to the death. In fact, the German command referred to this doctrine as the *An-sich-herankommen-lassen*, or "invitation-to-walk-right-in," system: attackers would be allowed to advance into the depths of the defense, where they would eventually be halted and repulsed by counterattack. The larger intention was still to retain ground in the end, but it was expected that the means to this end would be fluid, involving a heavy emphasis on movement and counterattack and discouraging decisive engagement in static defenses of specific points.[35] This is still a long way from the Viet Cong, but it was substantially less "conventional" than the Maginot Line.

German World War II defensive doctrine was still less "conventional." The German defenses opposing the British offensive in Operation GOODWOOD of July 1944, for example, were distributed over a depth of

---

35. See, e.g., G. C. Wynne, *If Germany Attacks: The Battle in Depth in the West*, London: Faber and Faber, Ltd., 1940; Greenwood Press reprint, 1976, pp. 191-318; Timothy Lupfer, *The Dynamics of Doctrine: Changes in German Tactical Doctrine During the First World War*, Ft. Leavenworth KS: U.S. Army Combat Studies Institute, 1981, Leavenworth Paper No. 4, pp. 1-36; Wilhelm Balck, *Development of Tactics, World War*, Harry Bell tr., Ft. Leavenworth, KS: The General Service Schools Press, 1922 trans. of 1920 orig., pp. 151-168; Ritter von Leeb, *Defense*, Stefan Possony and Daniel Vilfroy, trans., Harrisburg, PA: Military Service Pub. Co., 1943 trans. of 1938 orig., pp. 77-99.

more than 10 miles and built around a series of fortified French farming villages whose civilian buildings and outworks were exploited for concealment. Most of the defensive system's combat power was held in mobile reserve still further to the rear, and success rested on the assumption that the prepared positions would merely delay an attack while this large reserve maneuvered fluidly to its flanks for the counterattacks that were expected to halt the attacker; forward defenses were not expected to hold ground to the last cartridge, but were to break contact and withdraw if possible to reinforce other defenses to their rear.[36]

The U.S. defense of Saudi Arabia in Operation DESERT SHIELD of 1990 was even less like the Maginot Line. Here, a covering force of under 50,000 troops was expected to fight only a delaying action, withdrawing gradually through a zone of 80 miles depth without accepting decisive engagement, while setting the stage for a climactic action to be fought in a main battle area extending back to 150 miles from the frontier. On the critical coastal sector, a total defensive force of less than 170,000 troops was dispersed over more than 12,000 square miles (or an average density of under 15 soldiers per square mile), and was expected to fight a fluid, distributed action oriented largely to the enemy rather than the peculiarities of the ground.[37]

---

36. Biddle, *Military Power*, ch. 6.

37. Troop counts are taken from Eliot A. Cohen, Director, *Gulf War Air Power Survey*, Vol. V: *Statistical Compendium*, Washington, DC: U.S. Government Printing Office, 1993, p. 51, for the week ending October 31, 1990; dispositions are taken from U.S. Department of Defense, *Conduct of the Persian Gulf War*, Final Report to Congress Pursuant to Title V of Public Law 102-25, Washington, DC: U.S. Government Printing Office, April 1992, p. 40, and represent deployments as of "October 1990." The troop count in Cohen is for U.S. Army and Marine contributions; dispositions in the coastal sector include one Saudi Arabian

Other intermediate cases are usually thought of as "guerrilla" actions but display important features of conventional war fighting. The Tet Offensive of 1968, for example, combined raids by the Viet Cong with set-piece offensives by North Vietnamese army regulars as at Hue, Khe Sanh, and Saigon, which were intended to take and hold major Allied positions and involved sustained heavy combat for control of key terrain. The Communist attempt to overrun the fortified Marine base at Khe Sanh, for example, continued through more than 2 months of heavy fighting. North Vietnamese and Viet Cong forces actually captured Hue City and defended it against a sustained counterattack until driven out in a battle that resembled World War II urban warfare and lasted more than 3 weeks.[38]

Partisan warfare offers yet another intermediate case. Soviet partisan operations using lightly armed irregulars in mostly civilian clothing to raid German supply lines behind the combat front in the east during World War II employed tactics typically associated with guerrilla warfare, but did so on a vast scale and in the context of a mostly-conventional World War: Operation CONCERTO in September 1943, for example, employed over 200,000 partisan combatants to

---

infantry brigade and two Saudi mechanized battalions in the covering force zone; I assume a total of 7,000 soldiers for these, which is almost certainly an overestimate. I also assume an entire division personnel slice for each U.S. division shown in the sector, which is also an upper bound on actual strength in the defended zone. The troop density figures in the text above are thus highly conservative.

38. Keith William Nolan, *The Battle for Saigon: Tet 1968*, New York: Pocket Books, 1996; Nolan, *Battle for Hue: Tet 1968*, Novato, CA: Presidio Press, 1983; John Prados and Ray W. Stubbe, *Valley of Decision: The Siege of Khe Sanh*, Boston: Houghton Mifflin, 1991; James J. Wirtz, "The Battles for Saigon and Hue: Tet 1968" in Desch, *Soldiers in Cities*, pp. 75-87.

disrupt German rail traffic over a 900 by 400 kilometer zone.[39]

Intermediate points such as these characterize most actual historical warfare—the Maginot Line and the Viet Cong in 1965 are outliers in their extremity. The reality of military behavior is variance of degree along a continuum between uncommon extremes. The resulting differences are important—they can give rise to very different optimal military responses from the United States. But they are not easily captured by a simple dichotomy between "conventional" and "guerrilla" or "irregular," which conceals as much as it reveals, and creates a great deal of inevitable tension between the expectations created by the simple categories and the real behavior of actual militaries, few of whom conform to the categories' expectations very consistently.[40] To characterize any given military's

---

39. Kenneth Slepyan, *Stalin's Guerrillas: Soviet Partisans in World War II*, Lawrence, KS: University Press of Kansas, 2006; Alexander Hill, *The War Behind the Eastern Front: The Soviet Partisan Movement in North-West Russia, 1941-1944*, London: Frank Cass, 2005; Leonid D. Grenkevich, *The Soviet Partisan Movement, 1941-1944: A Critical Historiographical Analysis*, London: Frank Cass, 1999, pp. 223-272.

40. Of course, it is always possible to truncate a continuum at some arbitrary cutoff point and reduce it to a dichotomy. One could, for example, declare that anything less "conventional" than the Tet Offensive will be defined as "irregular" or "guerrilla" warfare and vice versa. Any continuum can be simplified into a set of discrete categories; the larger the number of categories, the closer the simplification approaches the continuous reality. To reflect the diversity of real military behavior, however, would require multiple intermediate categories, losing much of the benefit of the putative simplification. Some, however, have recently added a single intermediate category of "hybrid warfare": see, esp., Frank G. Hoffman, *Conflict in the 21st Century: The Rise of Hybrid Wars*, Arlington, VA: Potomac Institute for Policy Studies, 2007. The notion of "hybrid" war makes a valuable contribution in breaking down unhelpful dichotomies between "conventional" and "guerrilla," and is a clear and important step in the right

behavior thus requires a more discriminating analysis that parses behavior into its component parts, treats them independently, and identifies differences of degree in magnitude as well as differences of kind where these exist. We now turn to that assessment for Hezbollah in 2006, beginning with a brief outline of the key events of the campaign.

CAMPAIGN OVERVIEW

The 2006 Lebanon Campaign opened when Hezbollah ambushed an Israeli Defense Force (IDF) patrol and captured two Israeli soldiers on July 12.[41] The Israeli Air Force (IAF) quickly retaliated against targets

---

direction. Reliance on a single new category, however, poses conceptual problems. Hoffman sees "hybrid" wars as a novel form, yet strictly interpreted, his definition of "hybrid" encompasses almost all real historical warfare in this middle category: Hoffman defines "hybrid" wars as those involving conventional and irregular methods by the same units in the same battlespace (*ibid.*, e.g. pp. 8, 29). But as noted above, only the rare extrema involve *any* battlespace that lacks some aspects of both conventional and guerrilla methods—amalgams in the same time and space are the norm, not the exception. Hoffman does not explicitly define or bound the "conventional" and "irregular" categories in terms that enable unambiguous classification of cases (the monograph's discussion of the Lebanon case, for example, does not actually try to establish whether Hezbollah "conventional" units did or did not also employ "irregular" methods in the same battlespace or if so, how—the discussion focuses on the conventional features of the campaign). Hoffman at times implies, in fact, that all future warfare may converge on this hybrid model (p. 28, but cf. p. 43). We thus adopt a continuum here rather than a trichotomous "conventional-irregular-hybrid" simplification, but the latter is clearly an important improvement over the dichotomous treatment so common in the field.

41. Yaakov Katz, Herb Keinon *et al.*, "Eight IDF Soldiers Killed, 2 Kidnapped on Northern Frontier," *Jerusalem Post*, July 12, 2006; Harel and Issacharoff, *34 Days*, pp. 3-5; Blanford, "Deconstructing Hizbullah's Surprise Military Prowess."

in Lebanon. Before dawn on July 13, the IAF executed Operation SPECIFIC GRAVITY, destroying more than 50 of Hezbollah's long-range rocket launchers in a pre-planned, 34-minute strike.[42] Other early targets included Hezbollah observation posts along the border, Hezbollah compounds in the *Dahyia* section of Beirut, and roads and bridges that Israel believed might be used to exfiltrate the abducted soldiers. Over the course of the campaign, the IAF flew roughly 5,000 strike missions, primarily directed at the *Dahyia*, the Beqaa Valley near the Syrian border, and the region south of the Litani River. (See Figure 2.)[43]

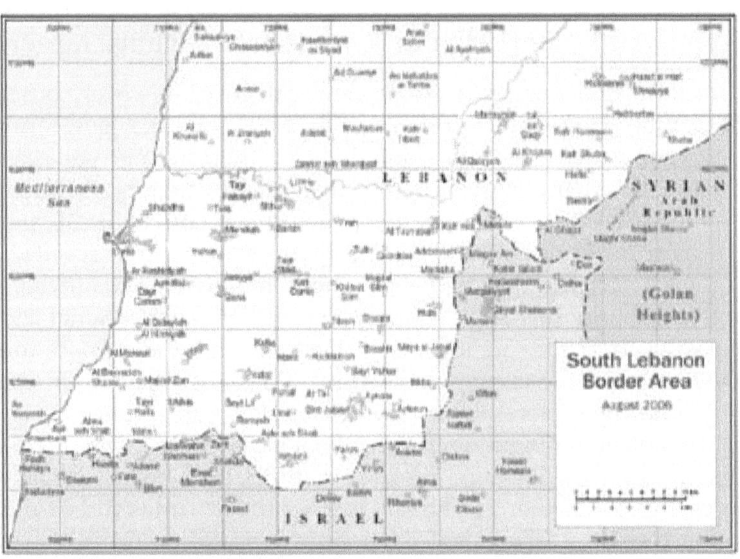

Credit: United Nations Cartographic Section.

Figure 2. Map of Southern Lebanon.

42. Arkin, *Divining Victory*, pp. 170-171; Rubin, *The Rocket Campaign*, p. 18; "Halutz: Mr. PM, We Won the War," *YNetnews.com*, August 27, 2006.

43. Arkin, *Divining Victory*, pp. 63, 73, and Appendix C.

Meanwhile, despite losing many of its long-range launchers early in the war, Hezbollah began what would become a steady stream of rocket fire into Israel. In total, Hezbollah fired an estimated 4,000 rockets, the vast majority of which were 122 mm Katyushas stationed within 20 kilometers of the Israeli border.[44] Hezbollah launched 100 or more rockets on 22 of 34 days in the campaign, including 220 on the final day of the war. About 900 of these rockets landed in urban areas, causing 53 civilian deaths.[45]

Israel made its first major ground incursion into Lebanon on July 19. IDF units advanced from the Israeli village of Avivim toward Marun ar Ras, a Lebanese town on high ground controlling much of the border area as well as the approach to the larger town of Bint Jubayl. The IDF met heavier resistance than they expected, including a protracted firefight at the Shaked outpost overlooking Marun ar Ras on July 19 and another battle inside the town on July 20.[46] When the IDF moved into Bint Jbeil, it encountered even tougher defenses, precipitating one of the largest firefights of the war on July 26.[47]

By the end of July, the IDF had conducted operations in several other towns close to the border, including Marwahin, Ayta ash Shab, Kafr Kila, and At Tayyibah, but it had made no attempt to control territory systematically in southern Lebanon. This changed on

44. Rubin, *The Rocket Campaign*, pp. 10-11; Arkin, *Divining Victory*, pp. 55-56, 59.

45. Rubin, *The Rocket Campaign*, pp. 10-15.

46. Winograd, *Final Report*, pp. 87-89; Shelah and Limor, *Captives in Lebanon*, pp. 161-165; Rapaport, *Friendly Fire*, pp. 145-147; Katz, "Heavy IDF Casualties in Firefight at Border," *Jerusalem Post*, July 21, 2006, p. 1.

47. Winograd, *Final Report*, pp. 111, 131; Shelah and Limor, *Captives in Lebanon*, pp. 187-191; Rapaport, *Friendly Fire*, pp. 198-199; Ed Blanche, "IDF Setback at Bint Jbeil," *Jane's Defence Weekly*, August 9, 2006.

July 31 when the Israeli Cabinet approved Operation CHANGE OF DIRECTION 8, designed to take and hold a "security zone" several kilometers wide along the entire border. The operation involved roughly 10,000 soldiers from eight brigades including, for the first time in the campaign, the deployment of reserves into combat.[48] By August 9, IDF forces were operating in almost every town along the border, pushing as far as Dibil in the south (4.5 km from Israel) and Al Qantarah in the northeast (7 km from Israel).[49]

On August 11, the IDF launched the final phase of the ground campaign, Operation CHANGE OF DIRECTION 11.[50] Described as a "push to the Litani," the main effort was actually a westward advance parallel to the river: an armored column from the 401st Brigade moved from At Tayyibeh toward Frun and Ghanduriyih (about 12 km west of Israel's northern tip) in order to link up with troops from the Nahal Brigade who had been airlifted into position.[51] As the 401st moved toward its objective through the Saluqi valley on August 12, it was ambushed with anti-tank guided missile (ATGM) fire; 11 tanks were hit, and 12 soldiers were killed.[52] Meanwhile, Hezbollah had regrouped in Ghanduriyih, leading to firefights in the town and

---

48. Winograd, *Final Report*, pp. 140-141; Ben-David, "Israel Re-Establishes 'Security Zone' in Southern Lebanon," *Jane's Defence Weekly*, August 9, 2006; Harel and Issacharoff, *34 Days*, p. 173; Makovsky and White, *Lessons and Implications of the Israel-Hizballah War*, p. 41.

49. Arkin, *Divining Victory*, p. 51; Blanford, "Deconstructing Hizbullah's Surprise Military Prowess."

50. Winograd, *Final Report*, pp. 201-205.

51. Ben-David, "IDF Conducts Massive Airlift Operation into Lebanon," *Jane's Defence Weekly*, August 23, 2006.

52. Winograd, *Final Report*, pp. 212-213; Shelah and Limor, *Captives in Lebanon*, pp. 395-396; Exum, *Hizballah at War*, p. 11; Harel and Issacharoff, *34 Days*, pp. 221-224.

its surrounding area throughout the final 2 days of the war.[53]

At 8 a.m. on August 14, Israel and Hezbollah implemented a United Nations (UN) Security Council ceasefire. By this time, the IDF had taken up ground positions in more than two dozen Lebanese towns, though a large portion of ground below the Litani—north of Al Mansuri and west of Ghanduriyih—had seen almost no IDF ground presence during the campaign.[54] In 34 days of fighting, the IDF had sustained 119 combat fatalities; Hezbollah had lost at estimated 650 to 750 fighters.[55]

HEZBOLLAH TACTICS IN LEBANON, 2006

Hezbollah's behavior has already been subject to a wide range of assessments, mostly on the basis of subjective judgments using ambiguous criteria, yielding a great deal of disagreement with limited prospects for closure. Our aim here is to provide a more replicable, objectively coded assessment with stronger potential for cumulation into a consensus view in the analytical community. To do this, we identify a series of directly observable, disaggregate variables corresponding to the key differences of kind and degree in the taxonomy above; we then code these variables for the Hezbollah case on the basis of direct observational evidence drawn chiefly from our interviews with IDF participants in the fighting. Together with the results of a similar process for theater strategy and operations, we then use the resulting codings to place Hezbollah on the spectrum presented in the taxonomy discussion above.

---

53. Winograd, *Final Report*, pp. 212-213, 217-218, 224; Shelah and Limor, *Captives in Lebanon*, pp. 395-396.

54. Arkin, *Divining Victory*, pp. 51-52.

55. This range is given in Arkin, *Divining Victory*, p. 74.

In particular, at the tactical level of war we code values for six variables relating to the degree to which the actor contests ground and accepts decisive engagement, and the manner in which concealment is sought:

- the duration of firefights;
- the proximity of attackers to defenders;
- the incidence of counterattack;
- the incidence of harassing fires and unattended minefields;
- the proximity of combatants to civilians; and
- the use of uniforms to distinguish combatants from civilians.

The Duration of Firefights.

Conventional defenders who seek to hold the ground they occupy must remain in position as long as they are under attack. Against a determined attacker, this can produce extended engagements or a series of renewed firefights in single locations. By contrast, classical guerrillas who seek only to inflict casualties at minimum cost and minimum risk to themselves rarely remain in place over extended durations, as this enables government forces to fix their locations and bring superior firepower to bear. Instead, classical guerrilla ambushes are brief, to enable the guerrillas to escape after a one-sided surprise volley of fire at an unsuspecting target. Of course, conventional defenders who are destroyed or broken quickly can fail to hold a position very long; conventional attackers who are destroyed or driven off quickly can terminate engagements early. Brief firefights can thus be observed in either the conventional or guerrilla extreme. But extended firefights over individual positions are inconsistent with an extremum of guerrilla tactics and suggest instead an attempt to hold ground. Hence the longer the observed duration of firefights, the greater the degree to which the actor's methods approximate the conventional extreme.

In Lebanon in 2006, Hezbollah defenders often engaged in very extended firefights—certainly far longer than one would expect from guerrillas with no intention of holding ground. At the Shaked outpost, for example, a dug-in Hezbollah defensive position remained in place on a critical hillcrest near the Israeli border between Avivim and Marun ar Ras, exchanging fire with IDF tanks and infantry for more than 12 hours before finally being destroyed in place by Israeli fire.[56] At Marun ar Ras, Hezbollah defenders held their positions through a 5-7 hour struggle with IDF attackers.[57] At Bint Jubayl, Hezbollah defenders fought a series of pitched battles over a period of more than 4 days, including individual firefights lasting as long as 8 hours, as on July 26, and 6 hours, as on July 28, and sporadic fighting continued in the town until the end of the war on August 14.[58] At Ghanduriyih, the fighting lasted for more than 2 days (August 12-14), including firefights of 7-8 hours at a time.[59] The battle for At Tayyibah on July 29-30 lasted 24 hours, including 4-5 hours of especially heavy fighting at close quarters.[60] Al Qantarah saw a 4-hour long engagement.[61] In the

56. 1LT O int., MHI:031308a1.

57. 1LT T int., MHI:031308p2; see also LTC N int., MHI:-031308p3.

58. MAJ S int., MHI:031708a3; COL H int., MHI:121817a; 1LT B int., MHI:031318a2.

59. LTC R int., MHI:121807p4; LTC A int., MHI:031608p3; COL M int., MHI:031608a1.

60. LTC S int., MHI:031608a2.

61. LTC A int., MHI:031608p3.

Saluqi valley, Hezbollah ATGM teams occupying a series of positions in depth received return fire from Israeli Merkava tanks after their initial launches, but stood their ground and continued to fire at least 10 additional missiles, ceasing fire and withdrawing only when IDF artillery was brought to bear.[62] Some engagements were shorter, but many were sustained over many hours or many days duration.[63]

The Proximity of Attackers to Defenders.

Conventional defenders who seek to hold the ground they occupy against an advancing attacker must also stand that ground even as the attacker closes with, and potentially reaches, their positions. By contrast, classical guerrillas who seek only to inflict casualties at minimum cost and minimum risk to themselves rarely allow superior government forces to close with them over any extended advance under fire. The risk of decisive engagement grows as an attacker closes with a defender; to allow an attacker into close proximity is to risk being unable to break contact and escape. Ambushes with an overwhelming concentration of fire delivered suddenly against an exposed target will sometimes be triggered at close range to maximize surprise and accuracy, but such tactics are risky for guerrillas and, when undertaken, must be concluded quickly. Frequent combat at close proximity, and especially, close proximity tolerated for more than a few minutes in a surprise ambush, thus

---

62. 1LT O int., MHI:031308a3.

63. The firefight at Haddatha on August 12, for example, lasted under 2 hours: MAJ K int., MHI:031608p2; the action at Rabb ath Thalathin on July 30 lasted about an hour: MAJ E int., MHI:031708a2. Not all engagements were of extended duration, but many were—far more than one would expect of a combatant with no intention of holding ground.

tends to imply behavior closer to the conventional end of the spectrum. Other things being equal, the greater the observed incidence of close-quarters fighting, the greater the degree to which the actor's methods approximate the conventional extreme.

In Lebanon in 2006, Hezbollah defenders frequently held their positions and continued to fire even after IDF attackers closed to very short ranges—often well within the bounds of decisive engagement for the defenders. The Hezbollah defensive position at Shaked, for example, was finally overrun in place by Israeli assault; the garrison's 20 fighters were all killed without any attempt at withdrawal or surrender over the course of a 12-hour battle.[64] Hezbollah defenses at Marun ar Ras and Bint Jubayl were similarly held until destroyed in close combat after extended advances to ranges of as little as 10-100 meters, with no apparent attempt to break contact or withdraw.[65] At Marun ar Ras, Aytarun, and Markaba, Hezbollah defenders held their fire until advancing IDF infantry had passed their outlying posts and were within the defense system itself, making withdrawal impossible.[66] At Bayt Yahun, Hezbollah defenders allowed Israeli tanks to drive by windows on the street below, opening small-arms fire against IDF armored vehicle commanders standing in open hatches at ranges of under 20 meters.[67] At Marun ar Ras, Hezbollah defenders fought literally room-to-room within buildings after IDF attackers had entered the structures.[68] At Ghanduriyih, defenders whose positions had been flanked but who retained potential

64. 1LT O int., MHI:031308a1.

65. COL H int., MHI:121817a; MAJ S int., MHI:031708a3; LTC O int., MHI:121607p; 1LT O int., MHI:031308a1; 1LT T int., MHI:031308p2.

66. 1LT O int., MHI:031308a1; 1LT Y int., MHI:031308p1.

67. 1LT Y int., MHI:031308p1.

68. 1LT T int., MHI:031308p2.

escape routes through the town nevertheless remained in position and were eventually destroyed in close combat; IDF attackers could make only 600 meters of progress in a day of hard fighting. Of the Hezbollah fighters, 57 dead bodies were recovered from the town.[69] At At Tayyibah, the Hezbollah garrison lost 20 of its 30 fighters in close combat before being ordered to withdraw.[70] At Aytarun, the defenders were withdrawn only when it became apparent that their position had become tactically irrelevant—the IDF had bypassed them, reaching Marun ar Ras from the southwest and rendering the blocking position at Aytarun moot.[71] At Haddatha, some 30 fighters remained in position in the village until the ceasefire, even after the IDF had nominally occupied the village.[72] There was thus a substantial volume of close-quarters combat in 2006; some of the defenders involved may have expected to annihilate the attackers by surprise safely at point-blank range, but in many of these cases, the defenders were accepting decisive engagement in the context of protracted firefights that are more consistent with an intent to hold ground.

The Incidence of Counterattack.

Conventional defenders who seek to hold ground must counterattack periodically to retake lost positions. Deliberately closing with the enemy in a counterattack,

---

69. LTC R int., MHI:121807p4; LTC A int., MHI:031608p3. Note that the survivors eventually withdrew in violation of orders to stand their ground: *ibid*.

70. LTC S int., MHI:031608a2.

71. 1LT O int., MHI:031308a1. See also LTC D int., MHI: 121807p3, on receiving fire from Hezbollah positions that had been previously bypassed throughout the theater.

72. MAJ K int., MHI:031608p2.

however, usually involves a greater degree of exposure than does a well-prepared defense. Classical guerrillas who seek one-sided attrition of the enemy but not the retention of ground thus make very sparing use of counterattack by maneuver. Hence the greater the observed incidence of counterattack, the greater the degree to which the actor's methods approach the conventional extreme.

Hezbollah did not routinely or uniformly counterattack when driven from positions, as German defenders, for example, typically did in World War II.[73] But there are multiple documented examples nevertheless of Hezbollah counterattacks in 2006. At Marun ar Ras on July 20, 15-30 Hezbollah fighters, advancing from the direction of Bint Jubayl, conducted a deliberate assault on an Israeli company position occupying a group of buildings on the crest of Hill 951. The Hezbollah attackers divided into two elements, supported by fire from a school building in the town east of the hill, striking the Israeli company simultaneously and by surprise, opening fire from a range of 40 meters, mounting multiple attempts after being beaten back initially, and eventually reaching hand-to-hand combat with the defenders.[74] At Bint Jubayl, a detachment of 40-60 fighters attacked Israeli defenses on Hill 850. The attackers were again divided into a main and secondary effort, with supporting ATGM fire from two directions

73. See, e.g, Timothy A. Wray, *Standing Fast: German Defensive Doctrine on the Russian Front During World War II: Prewar to March 1943*, Ft. Leavenworth, KS: U.S. Army Command and General Staff College, 1986, pp. 9-16; House, *Combined Arms Warfare in the Twentieth Century*, p. 163.

74. LTC N int., MHI:031308p3 and associated sketch map, MHI:031308p3m; COL H int., MHI:121817a. Note that COL H describes the school building as being to the north of Hill 951. For other instances of counterattacks at Marun ar Ras, see LTC A int., MHI:121608a.

and at least sporadic indirect fire support from remotely located mortar teams. The attack closed to within 10 meters of the Israeli positions before being driven off.[75] In the casbah at Ayta ash Shab, Hezbollah fighters assaulted, and succeeding in entering, a group of IDF-defended buildings.[76] At Muhaybib, 15-20 Hezbollah fighters assaulted IDF-defended buildings in groups of 3-4, operating on multiple axes, and supported by ATGM fire.[77] At Ghanduriyih, a single team of 3-5 fighters counterattacked the IDF after it had taken up positions in the casbah.[78] At Dayr Siryan, Hezbollah fighters assaulted Israeli positions from two directions with supporting fire from rocket propelled grenades (RPGs).[79] At Tayyibah on July 29, 10 Hezbollah fighters counterattacked after the IDF took the first in a line of Hezbollah-occupied houses, in an apparent attempt to retake the building.[80] In fact, there are many accounts of apparent counterattacks from across the theater; not all of these, however, can be distinguished unambiguously from confused movement toward undetected Israeli positions, ambush attempts, or other actions that may not have involved the intention to regain lost ground.[81]

75. On this and several other observed Hezbollah counterattacks in Bint Jubayl using multiple assault teams on multiple axes with supporting fire from ATGMs or mortars, see LTC N int., MHI:031308p3; COL H int., MHI:121817a; 1LT B int., MHI:031308a2. For a secondary account of this fighting, see Blanche, "IDF Setback at Bint Jbeil."

76. COL H int., MHI:121817a.

77. 1LT B int., MHI:031308a2.

78. LTC R int., MHI:121807p4. Hezbollah defenders at Ghanduriyih occupied a series of defensive lines disposed in depth; on several occasions when a line was taken, defenders would maneuver to the attackers' flanks in an apparent attempt to retake the positions: LTC A int., MHI:031608p3.

79. COL A int., MHI:122007p.

80. LTC S int., MHI:031608a2

81. See, for example, the accounts of actions at At Tayyibah, Aytarun, Haddatha (in which a small team of about five fighters

None of these actions, moreover, was at anything larger than platoon scale, and none succeeded in securing its territorial objective. But the engagements noted above were all unambiguous, deliberate attempts to close with Israeli defenders in positions recently taken by the IDF in ways that imply an intent to regain lost ground.

The Incidence of Harassing Fires and Unattended Minefields.

Conventional defenders seeking to hold ground by halting a determined attacker's advance require aimed fire in heavy volume. Minefields and other barrier systems can be of great assistance to any defender, but their ability to halt attackers is much reduced if the barrier is not overwatched by direct fire to interfere with clearance or avoidance. Aimed direct fire, however, requires an exposure to return fire. Guerrillas who do not seek to halt an advance outright but merely to inflict casualties can avoid return fire by striking from a safe distance with harassing indirect fires and unattended minefields, and will often prefer this. Harassing fires and unattended minefields can occur in any kind of conflict, but massed indirect fire and minefields or barriers tied in with direct fire overwatch are thus much more common in conventional than classical guerrilla warfare. Hence the greater the observed incidence of massed observed indirect fires and overwatched minefields, the greater the degree to which the actor's methods approximate the conventional extreme.

---

assaulted an IDF-occupied house on August 12, supported by fire from multiple directions; they successfully entered the building, killed an IDF soldier in an exchange of fire at very short range, and attempted to pull the body from the house before being driven off with the loss of at least four attackers), and Mays al Jabal in: COL A int., MHI:122007p; 1LT Y int., MHI:031308p1; MAJ K int., MHI:031608p2; LTC R int., MHI:121807p4.

Hezbollah in 2006 made considerable battlefield use of indirect fire, especially mortars, and had mined substantial stretches of southern Lebanon. But rarely was Hezbollah's mortar fire concentrated or intense. There were exceptions: at Markaba, for example, one IDF unit received at least 120 mortar rounds in the course of the assault.[82] And, of course, Hezbollah's rocket fire on Israeli civilian targets was heavy and sustained. Most battlefield mortar use, however, was accurate but light in volume and variable in its targeting.[83] Hezbollah minefield employment was sometimes tied into direct fire defensive systems in a systematic way and sometimes not. The defenses in Ghanduriyih, for example, included mines and obstacles overwatched by fires.[84] The main approach route up the Saluqi valley to the Litani River was mined and overwatched by well-concealed ATGM positions, requiring the IDF to undertake deliberate assault clearance by combined arms teams of combat engineers, tanks, and artillery.[85] Hezbollah defenses at Marun ar Ras were coordinated with elaborate mining of the main roadway at Junction 8; detonation of these explosives triggered the direct fire action in defense of the town on July 20.[86] Some minefields south of the Litani were organized to canalize IDF vehicles into open ground within range and in view of ATGM positions north of the river.[87] Yet the most extensive Hezbollah minefields could readily be bypassed, and Israeli combat engineers encountered

82. COL A int., MHI:122007p.

83. See, e.g., MAJ E int., MHI:031708a1; LTC A int., MHI:121607a; LTC R int., MHI:121807p4; 1LT O int., MHI:031308a1; LTC A int., MHI:031608p3; COL H int., MHI:121807a; LTC O int., MHI:121607a.

84. LTC R int., MHI:121807p4.

85. 1LT O int., MHI:031308a3.

86. LTC N int., MHI:031308p3.

87. COL M int., MHI:031608a1.

relatively few integrated barrier defenses requiring deliberate combat clearance under fire.[88] Booby traps were common, especially in and around abandoned houses, but little of the actual combat action took place through defended barrier systems, and massed indirect fires on assault forces in breaching operations were infrequent.[89]

The Proximity of Combatants to Civilians.

Classical guerrillas obtain much of their cover and concealment via intermingling with innocent civilians; classical conventional armies avoid civilians where possible and tend to obtain cover and concealment via terrain rather than civilian intermingling. Hence the greater the proximity of combatants to civilians, the greater the degree to which the actor's methods approximate the guerrilla extreme.

Hezbollah is often described as having used civilians as shields in 2006, and, in fact, they made extensive use of civilian homes as direct fire combat positions and to conceal launchers for rocket fire into Israel.[90] Yet the villages Hezbollah used to anchor its defensive system in southern Lebanon were largely evacuated by the time Israeli ground forces crossed the border on July 18. As a result, the key battlefields in the land campaign south of the Litani River were mostly

---

88. MAJ Z int., MHI:031608p4.

89. LTC R int., MHI:121807p4; COL M int., MHI:031608a1; MAJ E int., MHI:031708a1; LTC A int., MHI:121607p; 1LT B int., MHI:031308a2.

90. See, e.g., Erlich, *The Use of Lebanese Civilians as Human Shields*; Steven Erlanger and Richard A. Oppel, Jr., "A Disciplined Hezbollah Surprises Israel with its Training, Tactics and Weapons," *New York Times*, August 7, 2007, p. A8; "Israel's Dilemma after Qana," *Jane's Intelligence Digest*, August 4, 2006; Blanford, "Deconstructing Hizbullah's Surprise Military Prowess."

devoid of civilians, and IDF participants consistently report little or no meaningful intermingling of Hezbollah fighters and noncombatants. Nor is there any systematic reporting of Hezbollah using civilians in the combat zone as shields. The fighting in southern Lebanon was chiefly urban, in the built-up areas of the small to medium-size villages and towns typical of the region. But it was not significantly intermingled with a civilian population that had fled by the time the ground fighting began. Hezbollah made very effective use of local cover and concealment (see below), but this was obtained almost entirely from the terrain—both natural and man-made.[91]

The Use of Uniforms to Distinguish Combatants from Civilians.

Classical conventional militaries use uniforms or other distinguishing marks to differentiate combatants from noncombatants; classical guerrillas seek to blend in with civilians rather than to distinguish themselves from them, and hence often wear versions of typical ci-

---

91. See, e.g., LTC A int., MHI:121607a; COL H int., MHI:121817a; LTC R int., MHI:121807p4; COL A int., MHI:122007p; 1LT T int., MHI:031308p2; LTC N int., MHI:031308p3; MAJ S int., MHI:031608p1; MAJ E int., MHI:031708a1. There are reports of occasional exceptions. In Bint Jubayl, for example, a woman was seen waving a white flag from what was believed to be a Hezbollah-occupied house: LTC A int., MHI:121607a. "A few women" were spotted in At Tayyibah: LTC R int., MHI:121807p4. Some civilians were seen in Aytarun in the early days of the war, but not later: 1LT O int., MHI:031308a1. Isolated movement by civilian vehicles was reported in Haddatha: MAJ K int., MHI:031608p2. We heard no accounts, however, of any significant civilian population on any battlefield south of the Litani, or any systematic effort by Hezbollah to exploit civilian intermingling as a shield.

vilian clothing. Hence the greater the incidence of uniformed combatants, the greater the degree to which the actor's methods approximate the conventional extreme.

In 2006, the great majority of Hezbollah's fighters wore uniforms. In fact, their equipment and clothing were remarkably similar to many state militaries'—desert or green fatigues, helmets, web vests, body armor, dog tags, and rank insignia.[92] On occasion, IDF units hesitated to fire on Hezbollah parties in the open because their kit, from a distance, looked so much like IDF infantry's: at Addaisseh, seven Hezbollah fighters were mistaken for Israelis until an IDF soldier noticed that one of them was wearing track shoes.[93] Again, there were exceptions: at Marun ar Ras, most fighters were seen in uniform, but some armed combatants were also observed in civilian clothes; 2 of 20 bodies of dead Hezbollah fighters at At Tayyibah were found in civilian clothing; two fighters in civilian clothes were observed at Frun, and a few more at Al Qantarah; at At Tiri, combatants were observed in uniform pants, but not tops.[94] But the great majority of Hezbollah fighters in 2006 were uniformed and visually distinguishable from civilians.

---

92. See, e.g., LTC A int., MHI:121607a; COL H int., MHI:121817a; LTC R int., MHI:121807p4; COL A int., MHI:122007p; 1LT B int., MHI:031308a2; MAJ K int., MHI:031608p2; LTC A int., MHI:031608p3. Some Hezbollah fighters wore face paint for camouflage, further differentiating themselves from civilians: LTC R int., MHI:121807p4.

93. COL A int., MHI:122007p. Similarly, at Hill 951 at Marun ar Ras some IDF units were hesitant to fire on Hezbollah counterattackers because the latter looked so much like Israeli infantry: LTC N int., MHI:031308p3.

94. 1LT T int., MHI:031308p2; LTC S int., MHI:031608a2; MAJ E int., MHI:031708a1; LTC A int., MHI:031608p3; LTC I int., MHI:031708p.

HEZBOLLAH THEATER STRATEGY AND OPERATIONS IN LEBANON, 2006

Hezbollah's grand strategic objectives are a subject of considerable disagreement among Western analysts. Some see Hezbollah as an absolutist institution whose behavior reflects an uncompromising pursuit of aims centered on the destruction of Israel and the establishment of an Islamist theocracy across the region; tactics may vary, reflecting the limits of the possible at any given time, but in this view, the goals are fixed and very demanding.[95] Others see Hezbollah's goals themselves as more limited and pragmatic, focusing on consolidating its political standing in Lebanese domestic politics and modulating its conflict with Israel as necessary to suit its internal political needs.[96] Still others see Hezbollah in largely cultural terms, as a social movement whose behavior is shaped as much by theological or even self-expressive concerns—

95. See, e.g., Harel and Issacharoff, *34 Days*, pp. 259-260; Ely Karmon, *Fight on All Fronts: Hizballah, the War on Terror, and the War in Iraq*, Washington, DC: Washington Institute for Near East Policy Research Memorandum No. 45, December 2003, pp. 2, 6, 15-16; Eyal Zisser, "The Return of Hizbullah," *Middle East Quarterly*, Fall 2002.

96. See, e.g., Ahmad Nizar Hamzeh, *In the Path of Hizbullah*, Syracuse, NY: Syracuse University Press, 2004, pp. 80, 108-135, 144-146; Byman, "Should Hezbollah Be Next?" *Foreign Affairs*, Vol. 82, No. 6, November/December 2003, pp. 54-66; Byman, "Israel and the Lebanese Hizballah," in *Democracy and Counterterrorism: Lessons from the Past*, Robert J. Art and Louise Richardson, eds., Washington, DC: U.S. Institute of Peace Press, 2007, p. 322; Sami G. Hajjar, *Hizballah: Terrorism, National Liberation, or Menace?* Carlisle, PA: U.S. Army War College Strategic Studies Institute, 2002, p. 16; Adam Shatz, "In Search of Hezbollah," *New York Review of Books*, Vol. 51, No. 7, April 29, 2004, pp. 41-45; Judith Palmer Harik, *Hezbollah: The Changing Face of Terrorism*, London: I. B. Tauris, 2004, pp. 47-48; "Hizbullah's Islamic Resistance," *Jane's Terrorism and Security Monitor*, September 13, 2006.

as an embodiment of a religio-cultural striving for purification through conflict and struggle rather than as an instrumental means to some practical political or military end.[97]

For our purposes, however, the key issue is the degree to which its strategy for the conduct of the 2006 campaign per se was consistent with a classical guerrilla model or its conventional opposite. To establish this, we deduce from the taxonomy above four observable variables to be coded for the 2006 fighting:

- the balance of brute force and coercion;
- the relative concentration of combat power;
- the military organization of the theater of war; and
- the sensitivity of dispositions to the political orientation of the population.

The Balance of Brute Force and Coercion.

The conventional extreme at the strategic level of war relies heavily on brute force to seize or protect the disputed stake in the conflict without any voluntary decision to concede on the opponent's part. The guerrilla extreme, by contrast, is overwhelmingly coercive, manipulating the enemy's costs and benefits to induce the enemy to concede a stake that it could still seize or withhold if it chose. Coercion is widely employed,

97. See, e.g., Mona Harb and Reinoud Leenders, "Know Thy Enemy: Hizbullah, 'Terrorism' and the Politics of Perception," *Third World Quarterly*, Vol. 26, No. 1, February 2005, pp. 189-190; Amal Saad-Ghorayeb, *Hizbu'llah, Politics and Religion,* London: Pluto, 2002, p. 126; Naim Qassem, *Hizbullah: The Story from Within,* Dalia Khalil, trans., London: SAQI, 2005, pp. 39-40, 48-50; Dani Berkovich, *Can the Hydra Be Beheaded? The Campaign to Weaken Hizbollah,* Tel Aviv: Institute for National Security Studies, Memorandum No. 92, 2007 [In Hebrew], pp. 15-16. For a recent assessment of the role of culture in modern warfare generally, see Shultz and Dew, *Insurgents, Terrorists, and Militias.*

even by powerful actors in chiefly conventional wars; brute force, by contrast, is rarely encountered above the tactical level in classical guerrilla warfare. At the strategic level, an observation of coercive action per se is thus a relatively weak indicator of the difference between conventional and guerrilla methods, but the more extensive the role of brute force in conduct above the tactical level the greater the degree to which the actor's methods approximate the conventional extreme.

Hezbollah's military strategy in 2006, like its grand strategy, is disputed, and its representatives' stated views on this are insufficient to establish the intended role of coercion and brute force definitively. And unlike its tactics, Hezbollah's strategy cannot be determined unambiguously via the IDF interview data available to us. Its strategic intent thus cannot be observed directly. We can, however, deduce from Hezbollah's observed behavior at the tactical and operational levels a strategic logic consistent with that behavior, and exclude otherwise plausible alternative accounts, subject to the assumption that Hezbollah is an instrumentally rational actor (in the minimal, Clausewitzian sense that its actions are means to obtain political ends).

In particular, Hezbollah's observed behavior is consistent with a model in which a largely brute force pattern of operational art is designed to serve largely coercive strategic ends—a combination that falls short of the conventional extreme, but which is very common in great power warfare all the same. As a much weaker actor, Hezbollah surely understood that it could not destroy Israel or the IDF by force of arms in 2006. It also surely realized that Israel was capable of invading Lebanon and reestablishing or expanding upon its pre-2000 occupation. A preeminent requirement for any rational Hezbollah strategist would thus have been to design a means of deterring Israel from such a reoccupation, or coercing it into halting one should deterrence fail.[98] In principle, a variety of means for coercive pain infliction were available to Hezbollah; several of these options, however—and especially the use of suicide bombers—had been undermined by Israel's internal and border security policies. But rockets, which overfly border defenses and checkpoints, remained a powerful threat to Israeli population centers. Ideally, long-range launchers deployed in central or northern Lebanon would provide the needed coercive threat from locations beyond the reach of any plausible Israeli invasion. Long-range launchers, however, are large, distinctive, and relatively few in number, leaving them vulnerable to preemptive destruction by Israeli air strikes.[99] Shorter range rockets are smaller, easier to conceal, vastly greater in number, and potentially much less vulnerable to aerial preemption—but their range limited them to deployment in close proximity to the Israeli border and hence left them vulnerable to destruction by a ground invasion. This left Hezbollah with a dilemma: if they removed their chief coercive weapons from the reach of the Israeli Army, they would be vulnerable to the Israeli Air Force; if they used weapons survivable against the Air Force, they would be within reach of the Army.

The apparent solution to this dilemma was to rely chiefly on short-range rockets that could be concealed from air attack, but to protect these from ground invasion via a Hezbollah ground defense that would

98. Note that a plan for coercive pain infliction would be necessary even if Hezbollah calculated that a reoccupation would serve its domestic political interests: if it ultimately failed to inflict significant coercive pain on an Israeli occupier, its legitimacy in the eyes of its Shiite constituency would eventually collapse.

99. As demonstrated in the 2006 campaign by Israel's air strike in Operation SPECIFIC GRAVITY.

have to adopt a brute force operational doctrine of denying the IDF access to the launch areas.[100] Complete denial would be impossible—the IDF was, and is, too strong. But if a ground defense could hold long enough, it would enable ongoing rocket fire in the meantime to inflict mounting coercive pain on Israeli society. Retaliatory Israeli airstrikes, moreover, could be expected to inflame regional and world opinion, placing international political pressure on Israel to relent.[101] Neither of these coercive mechanisms, however, are quick—it takes time for political pressure

100. Some have argued that Hezbollah could solve this problem not by defending the launchers, but simply by deploying so many of them that the IDF could not possibly destroy them all. See, e.g., Rubin, *The Rocket Campaign*, pp. 26-27. It is far from clear, however, that this offered a practical solution without a credible, brute-force defense of southern Lebanon. To do this with long-range rockets fired from northern Lebanon, for example, would require saturating the Israeli Air Force's ability to destroy targets whose size makes them relatively easy for the IAF to find. Modern, high-technology air forces are very good at destroying exposed targets quickly and in large numbers; to acquire more targets than the IAF has munitions would be an extremely inefficient solution and would require Hezbollah to field an impractically large number of relatively scarce assets. To try this approach with short-range rockets, by contrast, is to assume that an unchallenged IDF ground invasion would not simply saturate the region with so many soldiers as to enable them to find even nominally hidden rockets quickly in large numbers. The IDF is large enough, and southern Lebanon is small enough, to have enabled Israel to do this if the cost of doing so were low; the whole logic of the analysis presented below is premised on the assumed need for Hezbollah to make this impossible by impeding the IDF's access to the launch areas.

101. Note that a short, intense air campaign of the kind needed to destroy Hezbollah long-range missile launchers could be concluded before such external political pressure would get very far. For external pressure to develop much leverage on Israel, a sustained campaign of extended duration would be required. Hezbollah may well have expected to profit politically from the

to build and for leverage on Israeli decisionmakers to mount; even a massive wave of rocket attacks would have little coercive effect if it were a short-term spasm with no prospect of longer-term continuation and escalation. The key operational-level requirement was thus to buy the time needed for the coercive campaign to succeed—to prevent the Israelis from getting quick access to the key launch areas on the scale needed to search the terrain exhaustively and uproot concealed rocket launchers before enough pressure could be built on the Israeli government to yield the issue at stake.

This operational requirement could not be met with classical guerrilla tactics, which allow enemy forces into the country but gradually penalize them for their presence with hit-and-run casualty infliction. Hezbollah could not preserve a system of hidden rocket launchers long enough for what might have to be thousands of individually small warheads gradually to build coercive pain if the IDF had ready access to the terrain in southern Lebanon. A brief incursion by tens of thousands of IDF soldiers might suffer a handful of losses to guerrilla ambushes, but in the meantime, it could roll up the entirety of Hezbollah's primary rocket force, end the coercive campaign against Israeli cities, then withdraw before its own casualties became prohibitive either. So Hezbollah set about the construction of a brute force defensive capability in southern Lebanon that might be able to delay an Israeli invasion long enough to enable a coercive strategy to succeed.

---

collateral damage inevitably associated with Israeli air operations, but if they based their strategy on long-range missiles alone this profit would have been slight. An ability to protract the campaign was essential for the success of any strategy involving external political pressure on Israel.

This analysis is broadly consistent with some assessments of Hezbollah's strategy in 2006.[102] But many have argued that Hezbollah intended its ground forces, as well as its rocket forces, to function coercively—as a classical guerrilla approach at both the strategic *and* the operational level in which the ground force role was to impose pain via IDF military casualties rather than to contest control of southern Lebanon.[103] And surely Hezbollah welcomed the coercive benefit of killing Israeli soldiers. But their observed behavior is inconsistent with a conclusion that this was the primary mission of Hezbollah's ground forces.

In particular, the tactics they actually employed in 2006 are much more consistent with an intention to hold ground than they are with an assumption that territorial control was unimportant and that their goal was the classical guerrilla aim of attrition per se. As we argue above, Hezbollah fighters defended positions too long, at ranges too short, and counterattacked too often, to square with a model of classical guerrilla intent. Nor did they exploit the potential of civilian intermingling in nearly the degree one would normally expect from a classical guerrilla force. This is not to say that Hezbollah's operational doctrine was one of Maginot-Line static defense, either—they accepted decisive engagement at some times and places but not others, they counterattacked to regain some lost ground but not all, they used mines and indirect fires to complement

---

102. In particular, Exum, *Hizballah at War*, p. 8; Romm, "A Test of Rival Strategies," pp. 58-59; Blanford, "Deconstructing Hizbullah's Surprise Military Prowess."

103. See, e.g., Kober, "The Second Lebanon War"; Kober, "The Israel Defense Forces in the Second Lebanon War," pp. 3-4; Siboni, "The Military Campaign in Lebanon," pp. 62-63; Rubin, *The Rocket Campaign*, pp. 26-27; Cody and Moore, "The Best Guerrilla Force in the World."

direct-fire territorial defenses in some places but as harassment tools in others. And their operational level intent appears to have been to delay rather than to hold indefinitely. Like most real militaries, Hezbollah's tactics were between the extremes. But their tactics were especially far from the guerrilla extreme. If their intent were merely to coerce Israel through the killing of IDF soldiers, they could have done so at much more advantageous loss-exchange ratios (and hence have continued such attrition longer, and killed more Israelis with the forces available to them) if they had *not* accepted decisive engagement by holding positions so long, or if they had *not* attempted counterattacks, or if they had persuaded civilians to remain under lower intensity combat and intermingled their fighters with the population. The tactical choices they made in 2006 are difficult to reconcile with an assumed intent to forgo brute force on the ground in favor of a classical guerrilla approach.

It is also possible that Hezbollah's strategy was the product of religio-cultural self-expression rather than an instrumentally rational plan to counter an Israeli threat via strategic coercion and operational brute force. A culture of struggle and resistance can be expressed in many ways; perhaps the observed pattern of tactics and operations is uniquely attributable to Hezbollah's particular belief system and world view. Following Lawrence, however, many have tended to associate Arab culture with guerrilla methods rather than conventional brute force.[104] Either way, it is clear that the ultimate result was a strategic program that at

104. See, e.g., T. E. Lawrence, *Seven Pillars of Wisdom*, London: Jonathan Cape, 1935, p. 224; Lawrence, "Twenty-Seven Articles," *The Arab Bulletin*, August 20, 1917; John Walter Jandora, *Militarism in Arab History*, Westport, CT: Greenwood Press, 1997, pp. 4, 8-9.

least mimicked a rationally instrumental design with considerable fidelity.[105]

It is important, though, not to attribute too much prescience or strategic foresight to Hezbollah in 2006. At a minimum, it is known that Hassan Nasrallah and the Hezbollah leadership were surprised by the severity of the Israeli response to the July 12 kidnapping; they had not anticipated this, and clearly had not intended war on this scale in 2006.[106] And it is far from clear that the war they found themselves in served their ultimate interests—they were widely perceived to have beaten Israel in the immediate aftermath, but in the process they suffered heavy military losses and their actions also brought a great deal of suffering on Lebanese civilians. In the longer run, this may or may not work out to their advantage.[107] Either way, the fighting that followed the kidnapping did not follow from any larger, integrated grand strategic plan—it emerged more organically from a series of miscalculations on both sides.

For Hezbollah, the 2006 campaign thus appears to have been the product of a fairly generic plan for the conduct of an unspecified future war with Israel,

---

105. For a similar argument on the apparent rationality of jihadi strategic thinking, see Brynjar Lia and Thomas Hegghammer, "Jihadi Strategic Studies: The Alleged Al Qaida Policy Study Preceding the Madrid Bombings," *Studies in Conflict & Terrorism*, Vol. 27, No. 5, September 2004, pp. 355-375.

106. See Herb Keinon, "No Second Round Looming," *Jerusalem Post*, August 28, 2006, p. 1; Matthew Schofield and Leila Fadel, "Regrets over Captures Aired," *Miami Herald*, August 28, 2006, p. A12.

107. For arguments that Hezbollah was not successful in the 2006 war, see Charles Krauthammer, "Hezbollah's 'Victory'," *Washington Post*, September 1, 2006, p. A21; Edward N. Luttwak, "Misreading the Lebanon War," *Jerusalem Post*, August 21, 2006, p. 13; Asher Susser, "Lebanon: A Reassessment," *Jerusalem Post*, September 13, 2006, p. 15.

which may or may not have been well-suited to the circumstances in which they found themselves, but could well have been the only plan available on short notice at the time. Most state militaries develop a variety of contingency plans for possible future conflicts, which they work out in peacetime, well in advance of an actual crisis, then shelve for possible future use. As such, they cannot anticipate the political particulars of the crisis that may bring war in any actual case. Ideally they are updated and adapted to the situation as it unfolds, but in Hezbollah's case, the 2006 war was a surprise, and Israel's quick escalation left them with little time for strategic adaptation. What they did have was a generic design and a series of elaborately prepared defensive works and rocket launch sites developed for that design. So they used what they had. The result was a coherent campaign at the tactical through theater level—and one that was in many respects more state-like and conventional than often expected from nonstate actors—but this campaign may or may not have ultimately served Hezbollah's larger grand strategic interests.

The Relative Concentration of Combat Power.

Classical guerrillas employ widely distributed forces at low, relatively uniform, densities; classical conventional armies operate in greater density and concentrate differentially at particular points. Hence the greater the relative concentration of combatants, the greater the degree to which the actor's methods approximate the conventional extreme.

Hezbollah in 2006 was more concentrated than some historical guerrilla forces, but fielded a smaller army for a theater the size of southern Lebanon than many historical conventional state militaries have.

Hezbollah's exact strength in 2006 is unknown, but Western estimates vary from a low of around 2,000 to a high of around 7,000.[108] Assuming a mid-range figure of 4,500, and given the area of Lebanon south of the Litani, this implies an average density of around 6 troops per square kilometer.[109] By contrast, the Viet Cong in 1964 fielded some 106,000 fighters across a country of 170,000 square kilometers, for a density of only one-tenth that of Hezbollah.[110] On the other end of the spectrum, the French in 1940 complemented the Maginot Line with 75,000 troops over 1,260 square kilometers, for a density 10 times that of Hezbollah.[111] And the U.S. defense of Saudi Arabia in 1990, as noted

108. For various estimates of Hezbollah's troop strength, see "Hizbullah," *Jane's World Insurgency and Terrorism*, June 26, 2007; Erlanger and Oppel, "A Disciplined Hezbollah Surprises Israel with Its Training, Tactics, and Weapons"; "Hizbullah's Islamic Resistance," *Jane's Terrorism & Security Monitor*, September 13, 2006; Anthony H. Cordesman, *Lebanese Security and the Hezbollah*, working draft, revised July 14, 2006, p. 25.

109. The area of Lebanon south of the Litani River is roughly 30 km by 25 km, or a total of 750 square kilometers. See map in Figure 2.

110. Viet Cong troop strength from Clodfelter, *Warfare and Armed Conflicts*, p. 740.

111. The Maginot Line was 140 km in length, and its fortifications were about 4 km in depth on average. The Line was also supported with artillery, including guns with a 27 km maximum range. We use the standard rule of thumb that artillery is generally positioned one-third of its range behind the front, and thus estimate that the average total depth of the Maginot Line defenses was 9 km. In 1940, France deployed 25 regiments of fortress infantry to the Line, at roughly 3,000 troops per regiment, for an estimated complement of 75,000. For these figures, see J.E. Kaufmann, *The Maginot Line: None Shall Pass*, Westport, CT: Praeger, 1997, pp. 57-58, 67, 85, 88; Vivian Rowe, *Great Wall of France: The Triumph of the Maginot Line*, New York: Putnam, 1959, p. 86.

above, deployed a density of around 5.5 troops per square kilometer, roughly equal to that of Hezbollah.[112]

The Military Organization of the Theater of War.

Classical guerrilla warfare is a relatively uniform, undifferentiated territorial defense without a distinguishable front or rear waged by guerrillas fighting largely where they live; classical conventional armies differentiate the theater into distinct covering force zones, main battle areas, rear areas and communication zones, sectors of main effort, and supporting or economy of force areas. Hence the more uniform or undifferentiated the military organization of the theater of war, the greater the degree to which the actor's methods approximate the guerrilla extreme.

Our ability to distinguish the theater-level military organization of southern Lebanon is limited by our lack of access to senior Hezbollah sources. We do know, however, that IDF ground forces entered some areas without resistance, whereas other locations were heavily—and apparently preferentially—defended. Rabb ath Thalathin, for example, was entered on July 30 without opposition.[113] Blida, Rshaf, Marjayoun, Marwahin, and Kafr Kila were all entered without receiving fire.[114] By contrast, villages such as Bint Jubayl, Marun ar Ras, Ghanduriyih, At Tayyibah, Muhaybib, Dayr Siryan, Aytarun, Bayt Yahun, Al Qantarah, and Markaba were all stoutly defended; the natural approach route through the Saluqi valley

---

112. See Footnote 37.

113. MAJ E int., MHI:031708a1.

114. 1LT T int., MHI:031308p2; LTC A int., MHI:121607a; MAJ J int., MHI:031508p; MAJ S int., MHI:031608p1; MAJ E int., MHI:031708a1.

was manned and contested.[115] Villages commanding key road junctions in the central part of the theater such as Bint Jubayl and Marun ar Ras were especially heavily defended, and key terrain commanding the approaches to these junctions, such as the Shaked outpost overlooking Marun ar Ras, was garrisoned and fortified.[116] The southwestern sector (An Naqurah to Ramyah), by contrast, offered less defensible terrain and appears to have been only lightly held.[117] Villages near the border with Israel were systematically better prepared for defense and more strongly manned than those in the interior.[118] Supplies and ammunition were stockpiled in locations commanding key terrain; other positions appear to have received little logistical prepositioning.[119]

115. See, e.g., 1LT T int., MHI:031308p2; LTC N int., MHI: 031308p3; MAJ S int., MHI:031708a3; COL H int., MHI:121817a; LTC R int., MHI:121807p4; LTC S int., MHI:031608a2; LTC A int., MHI:031608p3.

116. See, e.g., 1LT O int., MHI:031308a1; COL H int., MHI: 121817a; MAJ S int., MHI:031708a3; 1LT T int., MHI:031308p2; LTC N int., MHI:031308p3; 1LT B int., MHI:031308a2.

117. LTC D int., MHI:121807p3; LTC A int., MHI:121607a; MAJ S int., MHI:031608p1. Some, however, have attributed the lighter resistance encountered in the southwest to superior IDF tactics employed by the units operating there: MAJ J int., MHI:031508p.

118. LTC R int., MHI:121807p4.

119. In Bint Jubayl, Marun ar Ras, Muhaybib and elsewhere, for example, extensive stocks of ammunition, weapons, food and water were discovered, sufficient for weeks of combat without resupply: see, e.g., LTC A int., MHI:121607a; 1LT B int., MHI:031308a2; MAJ K int., MHI:031608p2. Bint Jubayl was contested through the end of the campaign with no apparent supply difficulties for the Hezbollah garrison. By contrast, Beit Yaroun was subject to much less extensive fighting, yet by the end of the campaign, Hezbollah fighters were observed moving from house to house searching for food; Hezbollah supplies had apparently run out, and no unconsumed prestocks of food or ammunition were observed in the village following its capture: MAJ S int., MHI:031608p1.

Perhaps most important, Hezbollah exercised a degree of hierarchical, differentiated command and control over subunits operating in key areas during the campaign, making apparent decisions to favor some sectors over others, hold in some places but yield in others, counterattack in some locations but withdraw elsewhere. A formal chain of command operated from designated and well-equipped command posts; used real time communications systems including landline cables and encrypted radio; issued orders; changed plans; and moved some elite units over considerable distances from rearward reserve areas to reinforce the key battle for the communications network in the central sector.[120] (See Figures 3 and 4.)

Credit: IDF.

Figure 3. Captured Hezbollah Communications Equipment, including Encryption Systems.

120. See, e.g., LTC N int., MHI:031308p3; MAJ J int., MHI: 031508p; COL M int., MHI:031608a1; MAJ K int., MHI:031608p2; MAJ E int., MHI:031708a1; COL H int., MHI:121817a; LTC S int., MHI:031608a2; LTC A int., MHI:031608p. Hezbollah also appears to have devoted considerable effort to intercepting IDF communications, though it is unclear whether they proved able to exploit any such intercepts: MAJ S int., MHI:031608p1; COL M int., MHI:031608a1; MAJ K int., MHI:031608p2.

Credit: IDF.

Figure 4. Hezbollah Outpost along the Lebanese-Israeli Border.

The scale of differentiation and articulation should not be exaggerated—much of the Hezbollah defense was static; reserve movements were very small scale; Hezbollah commanders rarely succeeded in adapting to changing conditions quickly or responsively; and Hezbollah's limited freedom to maneuver under Israeli air supremacy made any large-scale integration for mobile defense at the theater level impossible even if Hezbollah would have attempted this otherwise. But neither were their dispositions in southern Lebanon an undifferentiated territorial defense without distinctions between front and rear, or main effort and economy of force; the theater of war was clearly articulated for military purposes into differentiated sectors of operations with distinctions in emphasis and role.

The Sensitivity of Dispositions to the Political Orientation of the Population.

Classical guerrillas require logistical support and safe haven from a sympathetic population to fight effectively; classical conventional armies maintain specialized logistical systems separate and distinct from the population and the civil economy. Hence the greater the degree to which any nonuniformities in combat dispositions correlate with ethnic, sectarian, or other political demographic distinctions, the greater the degree to which the actor's methods approximate the guerrilla extreme.

Again, there are limits to what can be known, in this case due partly to the absence of interview evidence from Hezbollah senior leadership and partly due to limitations in what can be known about the sectarian and political demography of southern Lebanon. The latter is politically very sensitive, hence no census has been conducted in the region since 1932.

Nevertheless, there is some reason to believe that Hezbollah's dispositions and performance may have been influenced by the political orientation of the local population, and especially by the geographic distribution of Christians and Shiites. Historically, the northeastern sector near Metulla and Marjayoun had been heavily Christian, whereas the central part of the theater around Bint Jubayl and Marun ar Ras had been predominantly Shiite. Although there were some Hezbollah defenses in the northeast, this sector was less heavily defended than elsewhere.[121] This may have reflected the difficulties in making systematic defensive preparations amid an unsupportive population—

121. MAJ S int., MHI:031608p1; COL M int., MHI:031608a1; MAJ E int., MHI:031708a1.

and especially, in keeping those preparations covert and hidden from Israeli intelligence and target acquisition.[122] By the same token, however, most Lebanese villages were evacuated prior to the IDF's arrival, which would have enabled Hezbollah fighters to dispose themselves for combat without observation by any significant Christian civilian population even in the northeast. It is also unclear whether the inherent military value of the northeast for Hezbollah equaled that of the central region, with its critical road network and closer proximity to the major Israeli coastal cities to the southwest. The relationship between Hezbollah's conduct of the campaign and the political demography of southern Lebanon is thus unclear, but it is difficult to exclude some possibility of a connection.

HEZBOLLAH PROFICIENCY OF EXECUTION IN LEBANON, 2006

A final important distinction concerns Hezbollah's proficiency of execution. Inept performance is possible whether one attempts conventional or guerrilla methods; the former, however, is especially hard to do well without a great deal of specialized and perishable skills. Guerrillas, too, benefit from skilled execution, but guerrillas can get by with simple, unsophisticated hit-and-run methods that can be executed with minimal training. Competent conventional warfare at the theater level demands intensive training, especially for the coordination and synchronization of large-scale maneuver. An important reason for the commonplace intuition that nonstate actors cannot wage conventional warfare and will resort to irregular methods instead is

122. MAJ J int., MHI:031508p.

the expectation that the former demands skills beyond the reach of any but wealthy state militaries. Any organization can *attempt* to execute the conventional tactics and operational art often associated with interstate warfare; to do so *proficiently*, by contrast, is much more difficult.

Credit: IDF.

Figure 5. Hezbollah Bunker Entrance.

Hezbollah's proficiency of execution in 2006 was uneven. Some things were done very well. The selection, layout, and concealment of fighting positions, for example, were systematically very effective. IDF attackers were rarely able to identify Hezbollah combat positions prior to drawing fire from them, even from very short ranges. In Dayr Siryan, Israeli infantry approached to within 50-100 meters of Hezbollah fighters without spotting them; in Aytarun, tanks passed directly beneath the windows used to fire upon them without seeing the defenders first; in Bint Jubayl, defensive positions in buildings were still invisible to infantry advancing up directly adjoining streets; in At Tayyibah, Hezbollah defenders opened fire undetected from a range of 50 meters.[123] Movement among alternate and supplementary positions within buildings often enabled urban defenders to remain concealed even after extended firing; especially in villages near the Israeli border, tunnels were dug between buildings to facilitate concealed movement.[124] In the border area, combat preparations initiated years before the war resulted in civilian homes whose very construction was influenced by military tactical considerations: buildings in key locations were discovered with thicker, reinforced walls on the sides facing likely approach routes from Israel.[125] Other indoor combat positions near the border had sandbags or other reinforcements hidden in the interior to strengthen walls facing intended engagement areas.[126] Outdoor and rural

---

123. COL A int., MHI:122007p; 1LT Y int., MHI:031308p1; MAJ S int., MHI:031708a3; LTC S int., MHI:031608a2. For other examples from Bint Jubayl, Marun ar Ras, Mays al Jabal, Aytarun, and elsewhere, see, e.g., COL H int., MHI:121817a; LTC R int., MHI:121807p4; 1LT T int., MHI:031308p2; 1LT O int., MHI:031308a1; MAJ Z int., MHI:031608p4; LTC A int., MHI:031608p3. Of course, there were exceptions. In Haddatha, IDF intelligence learned of a Hezbollah position and a ground unit then spotted them moving around in a building: 1LT T int., MHI:031308p2. In Bayt Yahun, IDF ground forces identified a Sagger position in a house, and one mobile Sagger outdoors, and killed both before the crews realized they had been seen: MAJ S int., MHI:031608p1. In Ghanduriyih, many positions were concealed, but some could be identified prior to contact: cf. LTC R int., MHI:121807p4, and LTC A int., MHI:031608p3. But these exceptions were unusual. In most engagements, Hezbollah defenders got the first shot from positions that had not been identified beforehand.

124. See, e.g., LTC A int., MHI:121607a; LTC R int., MHI: 121807p4.

125. At Bint Jubayl, for example, reinforced walls facing the Israeli border remained standing after the rest of the structures had been destroyed: 1LT B int., MHI:031308a2.

126. See, e.g., COL H int., MHI:121817a; LTC A int., MHI:121607a; LTC R int., MHI:121807p4; LTC N int., MHI:031308p3. Note that while there is some evidence of similar preparations elsewhere

positions were sometimes very elaborately prepared, with concrete dugouts, multiple chambers, concealed entry and exit points, and carefully camouflaged firing positions; illustrative examples are depicted in Figures 5 to 7.[127] Antitank missile positions were especially difficult to locate, given the often extended range of ATGM engagements and Hezbollah's success at concealing launchers and crews (see Figure 8).[128] Terminal defenses for rural Katyusha rocket launch areas, dubbed "nature preserves" by the IDF, were especially intricate, well-camouflaged, and carefully prepared—sometimes including hydraulically raised and lowered launch tubes, concrete-reinforced caches, showers for garrisons, multiple entrances and exits, and interconnected outworks to enable concealed movement within the system (see Figures 9 to 11).[129]

(for Ghanduriyih, for example; see LTC R int., MHI:121807p4), interior positions in villages remote from the border were typically less extensively prepared: see, e.g., COL A int., MHI:122007p; MAJ K int., MHI:031608p2. Even some border-area positions appear to have been more hastily prepared, as with some buildings at Marun ar Ras (1LT T int., MHI:031308p2; or Mays al Jabal, cf. LTC R int., MHI:121807p4 and MAJ E int., MHI:031708a1), and in few cases were even better-prepared buildings fitted with loopholes, razor wire, or interior obstacles; Hezbollah urban defensive techniques were thus variable across the theater, and often not as extensive as in some other historical urban warfare—though the net results typically afforded Hezbollah defenders very effective concealment prior to, and often subsequent to, the exchange of fire.

127. See, e.g., 1LT O int., MHI:031308a1; LTC A int., MHI: 121607a.

128. See, e.g., 1LT O int., MHI:031308a3; COL M int., MHI: 031608a1; MAJ Z int., MHI:031608p4; 1LT Y int., MHI:031308p1; MAJ E int., MHI:031708a2.

129. LTC D int., MHI:121807p3.

Credit: IDF.

Figure 6. Hezbollah Bunker Entrance.

Source: Reuven Erlich, *The Use of Lebanese Civilians as Human Shields*, Gelilot: Center for Special Studies/Intelligence and Terrorism Information Center, 2006, p. 42.

Figure 7. Hezbollah Outdoor Firing Position.

Source: Reuven Erlich, *The Use of Lebanese Civilians as Human Shields*, Gelilot: Center for Special Studies/Intelligence and Terrorism Information Center, 2006, p. 92.

Figure 8. Hezbollah Kornet ATGM Position at Ghanduriyih.

Note that when loaded for firing, the missile would be fixed in a launch tube just above the guidance package shown; only the optics and the tube would be visible above the mask, providing an exposed cross section of under two feet square to be detected by targets multiple kilometers away.

Credit: IDF.

Figure 9. Hezbollah Rocket Launcher in Concealed Rural Position.

Credit: IDF.

Figure 10. Hezbollah Bunker Interiors.

Credit: IDF.

Figure 11. Hezbollah Bunker Entrance Stairs.

Hezbollah fire discipline was strong and consistent. Engagements were typically initiated by Hezbollah with coordinated, concentrated fire from multiple locations. Defenders routinely allowed lead echelons to pass, opening fire on follow-on elements once larger formations had advanced into kill zones; locations were rarely given away by premature firing from nervous individuals.[130]

Hezbollah effectively coordinated direct fires in support of its counterattacks, often from multiple directions.[131] Barriers and overwatching ATGM positions were sometimes integrated with considerable skill over multikilometer distances: east of Ghanduriyih, for example, a series of minefields were placed in locations that canalized Israeli columns into engagement areas exposed to ATGM fire from concealed launchers located north of the Litani River some five kilometers away.[132] And Hezbollah mortar fire was consistently accurate and responsive.[133]

Other things were done much less well. In particular, Hezbollah demonstrated no ability to control or coordinate the maneuver of large formations. Counterattacks, for example, never exceeded platoon strength, and many were considerably smaller, with individual maneuver elements sometimes as small as 3-5 soldiers; deliberate retrograde movements were

130. See, e.g., LTC D int., MHI:121807p3; 1LT O int., MHI: 031308a1; COL H int., MHI:121817a.

131. See, e.g., COL H int., MHI:121817a; MAJ S int., MHI: 031708a3; 1LT B int., MHI:031308a2; LTC N int., MHI:031308p3; MAJ K int., MHI:031608p2.

132. COL M int., MHI:031608a1.

133. See, e.g., LTC A int., MHI:121607a; LTC R int., MHI: 121807p4; 1LT O int., MHI:031308a1; LTC A int., MHI:031608p3; MAJ E int., MHI:031708a1 (though some felt Hezbollah's mortar marksmanship, though good, was actually stronger in the 1990s: COL H int., MHI:121817a).

normally limited to handfuls of combatants at a time; small detachments often fought isolated actions; and whereas perhaps 60-100 commandos were moved over great distances, no large reserve was withheld or maneuvered to counterconcentrate against IDF movements, and movements of Hezbollah forces within their forward defenses were small-scale and over short distances.[134] This should be kept in context: the entire size of the Hezbollah combatant force in southern Lebanon was probably well under 7,000, or less than the strength of two U.S. Army brigades—hence battalion- or brigade-size maneuver would be unrealistic. But the scale of maneuver attempted by Hezbollah in Lebanon was nonetheless very small by Western standards.[135]

Hezbollah demonstrated only limited combined arms cooperation. They frequently used ATGMs in concert with small arms and heavy machine guns in direct fire, and they made significant use of mortars—but rarely were direct and indirect fires combined against single targets or in single engagement areas. There were exceptions: at Bint Jubayl, for example, a Hezbollah counterattack combined direct fire support with suppressive indirect fire from remotely located mortars, which continued as Hezbollah ground forces advanced; at At Tayyibah on July 28-29, IDF units simultaneously received ATGM and mortar fire, each from ranges of multiple kilometers; at Ghanduriyih, IDF attackers similarly received simultaneous ATGM and mortar fire; the Israeli advance through the Saluqi

134. COL H int., MHI:121817a; COL M int., MHI:031608a1; 1LT B int., MHI:031308a2; LTC N int., MHI:031308p3; LTC S int., MHI:031608a2; MAJ K int., MHI:031608p2.

135. The authors are indebted to Yuri M. Zhukov for this observation. On Hezbollah troop strength in southern Lebanon, see note 107 above.

valley had to clear minefields under ATGM fire.[136] Such exceptions were uncommon, however. And Hezbollah showed no ability to orchestrate mines, obstacles, direct and indirect fire in a single, synchronized defense, or to do so over any extended defensive front.[137]

Few Hezbollah units showed much apparent ability to react to changing conditions. Counterattackers taken under surprise fire from previously concealed IDF positions away from the assault objective, for example, often halted and fell back in disorder rather than reorienting to the new threat, redirecting suppressive fire, and continuing the advance. Where Hezbollah organized linear defenses these were often flanked by Israeli attackers; the defenders, however, typically either fought on in the same positions or simply withdrew, rather than forming a new front to meet the assault. Although Hezbollah made apparent attempts to monitor Israeli communications networks, some of which (such as medical evacuation nets) operated in the clear, there is no evidence they were able to exploit any information gained.[138]

Hezbollah direct fire marksmanship was very uneven. Small arms fire, for example, was systematically inaccurate and caused few casualties.[139] Hezbollah ATGM crews, by contrast, could strike targets from extraordinary ranges: Israeli armored vehicles were regularly hit by missiles fired from 4-5 kilometers away.

---

136. COL H int., MHI:121817a; LTC S int., MHI:031608a2; 1LT O int., MHI:031308a3; COL M int., MHI:031608a1.

137. See, e.g., MAJ K int., MHI:031608p2; LTC N int., MHI: 031308p3; LTC A int., MHI:121607p; 1LT B int., MHI:031308a2; MAJ E int., MHI:031708a2; 1LT O int., MHI:031308a3.

138. See, e.g., 1LT B int., MHI:031308a2; LTC A int., MHI: 121607a; COL H int., MHI:121817a.

139. See, e.g., MAJ J int., MHI:031508p; LTC R int., MHI:121807p4.

Hezbollah frequently fired such missiles in salvos at single targets, however, and IDF armored vehicles normally maneuvered evasively and used smoke for obscuration once under attack. The result of this combination was that the ratio of ATGM hits to total launches could be very low. In the Saluqi valley fighting, missiles were fired in volleys of perhaps a dozen rounds at a time, of which 1-2 would hit their targets; an IDF combat engineering battalion in Ghanduriyih received 6-8 ATGM launches while maneuvering at night with no hits; on the night of August 12 outside At Tayyibah, a formation of more than 15 tanks received over a dozen *Kornets* fired from the village of Yuhmur, north of the Litani River roughly five kilometers away, suffering three hits, all of them against stationary vehicles—no moving targets were hit; in another engagement at At Tayyibah, one of a volley of four *Saggers* hit an IDF D9 armored bulldozer; the survivors popped smoke, but Hezbollah continued firing without further success.[140] The net result was a potentially lethal threat, but a very large expenditure of missiles per target struck.[141]

---

140. 1LT O int., MHI:031308a3; MAJ Z int., MHI:031608p4; MAJ E int., MHI:031708a2.

141. Some sources have estimated hit rates as low as 8 percent of all missiles fired for Hezbollah ATGMs: Ben-David, "ATGM Threat Poses Quandry for IDF Armour," *Jane's Defence Weekly*, August 16, 2006; Blanche, "Hizbullah ATGMs Take Heavy Toll in Lebanon," *Jane's Missiles and Rockets*, September 1, 2006. Estimated penetration rates per hit as reported in public sources vary from 20-45 percent: Erlanger and Oppel, "A Disciplined Hezbollah Surprises Israel with its Training, Tactics and Weapons," Ben-David, "Israeli Armour Fails to Protect MBTs from ATGMs," *Jane's Defence Weekly*, August 30, 2006. On balance, the result was low per-round efficiency, but high aggregate lethality, accounting for over 50 of the IDF's 119 fatalities: Blanford, "Deconstructing Hizbullah's Surprise Military Prowess."

CONCLUSIONS AND IMPLICATIONS

Hezbollah in 2006 thus conformed to neither ideal model. It was not a classical guerrilla army: it put too much emphasis on holding ground; it sought concealment chiefly via terrain rather than through civilian intermingling; its forces were too concentrated; and it appears to have articulated a differentiated theater of war for the purpose of defending rocket launch sites to be used in a strategic bombing campaign against Israeli population centers. But neither did it approximate a pure conventional extreme: its defense of ground was too yielding; it relied too extensively on harassing fires and unattended minefields; it put too much emphasis on coercion; and it may have disposed its forces too much in accordance with the population's political orientation.

But few real militaries conform perfectly to either classical ideal. The real issue is always their relative placement on a continuum. And Hezbollah's position on the guerrilla-conventional continuum in 2006 was much closer to the conventional end of the scale than nonstate actors are normally expected to be. In fact, Hezbollah was in many ways as "conventional" as some state actors have been in major interstate warfare. Hezbollah's relative emphasis on coercion was no greater, for example, than the North Atlantic Treaty Organization's (NATO) in 1999, Japan's in 1944, Nazi Germany's in 1944, or Wilhelmine Germany's in 1917; in military terms, Hezbollah's use of a ground force to secure base areas for the projection of strategic bombing into an enemy homeland is similar in certain respects to the U.S. island-hopping campaign in the Pacific in World War II, in which U.S. Army and Marine ground forces were used to secure runways from which bombers could strike Japanese cities.[142] Hezbollah's emphasis on ground force delay to enable such strategic strikes to secure its stakes bears a strong family resemblance to NATO's Cold War strategy of delaying a Soviet conventional invasion long enough for NATO nuclear escalation to coerce a halt to the attack.[143] Hezbollah's lack of sizeable reserves and heavy allocation of forces to forward, prepared defenses are similar to Germany's dispositions on the Seventh Army front opposite the U.S. offensive in Operation COBRA of July 1944: much as the German Commanding General Paul Hausser assumed that extensive reserve movement would be futile given Allied command of the sky, so Hezbollah appears to have concluded that Israeli air supremacy mandated a heavy allocation of effort to fixed defenses of key urban road junctions near the Israeli border.[144]

None of this is to afford to Hezbollah the moral or political legitimacy of NATO during the Cold War

---

142. Obviously there are many differences, too: U.S. forces were on the tactical offensive in the Pacific, Hezbollah was mostly on the tactical defensive; the Pacific campaign was amphibious and maritime, the 2006 fighting was continental; the U.S. campaign occurred in a war begun by an expansionist Japan, the Hezbollah campaign was waged in a war started by a Hezbollah kidnapping of Israeli soldiers on Israeli soil; and so on. But both campaigns involved the use of ground forces to secure bases for aerial coercion of an opponent via attacks on enemy cities, a concept not normally associated with guerrilla warfare. On the Pacific island hopping campaign, see, e.g., Philip A. Crowl, *The U.S. Marines and Amphibious War: Its Theory and Practice in the Pacific*, Princeton: Princeton University Press, 1951.

143. See, e.g., David Schwartz, *NATO's Nuclear Dilemmas*, Washington, DC: Brookings, 1983; J. Michael Legge, *Theater Nuclear Weapons and the NATO Strategy of Flexible Response*, Santa Monica: RAND, 1983, RAND R-2964-FF.

144. On German defenses opposite Operation COBRA, see Martin Blumenson, *Breakout and Pursuit*, Washington, DC: Office of the Chief of Military History, 1961, pp. 224-228, and Map V.

or the United States in World War II. But the military means Hezbollah used to pursue its ends in 2006 bore closer resemblance to state practices than many have supposed.

In fact, in many ways the greatest divergence between Hezbollah's military behavior in 2006 and that assumed for great power militaries in interstate warfare may have been the proficiency with which Hezbollah executed its doctrine, rather than the doctrine it was trying to execute. Hezbollah did some things well, such as its use of cover and concealment, its preparation of fighting positions, its fire discipline and mortar marksmanship, and its coordination of direct fire support. But it also fell far short of contemporary Western standards in controlling large-scale maneuver, integrating movement and indirect fire support, combining multiple combat arms, reacting flexibly to changing conditions, and small-arms marksmanship. Hezbollah appears to have *attempted* a remarkably conventional system of tactics and theater operational art, but there is a difference between trying and achieving, and in 2006 at least, Hezbollah's reach in some ways exceeded its grasp.

Yet Hezbollah is hardly alone in this. Many state actors have fallen far short of today's Western standards of military proficiency, both in today's world and historically. Saddam's "elite" Iraqi state Republican Guard, for example, proved systematically incapable of integrating movement and indirect fire support, combining multiple combat arms, reacting flexibly to changing conditions, and consistently hitting targets with either small *or* large caliber weapons; in two wars with the United States, the Iraqi state military's use of cover and concealment, combat position preparation, and fire discipline were consistently far *less* proficient than Hezbollah's.[145] The Italian state military in 1941 proved much less proficient in conventional warfare than did Hezbollah in 2006; French defenses on the critical Sedan front in 1940 were more exposed and no more able to react to changing conditions than Hezbollah's.[146] The Egyptian state military proved systematically less adept than Hezbollah in cover and concealment and little better than Hezbollah in coordinating large scale maneuver with combined arms or flexibly responding to changing conditions in 1956 or 1967; the Syrian state military did no better in 1967, 1973, or 1982.[147] In fact, Hezbollah inflicted more Israeli casualties per Arab fighter in 2006 than did any of Israel's state opponents in the 1956, 1967, 1973, or 1982 Arab-Israeli interstate wars.[148] Hezbollah's skills

145. See, esp., Stephen Biddle, "Speed Kills: Reevaluating the Role of Speed, Precision, and Situation Awareness in the Fall of Saddam," *Journal of Strategic Studies*, Vol. 30, No. 1, February 2007, pp. 3-46; *idem.*, "Victory Misunderstood: What the Gulf War Tells Us About the Future of Conflict," *International Security*, Vol. 21, No. 2, Fall 1996, pp. 139-179.

146. See, e.g., ISO Playfair *et al., The Mediterranean and Middle East, Vol. I: The Early Successes against Italy*, London: Her Majesty's Stationery Office, 1954; Allan R. Millet and Williamson Murray, *Military Effectiveness, Vol. III: The Second World War*, London: Unwin Hyman, 1991, pp. 136-179; Robert Doughty, *The Breaking Point: Sedan and the Fall of France, 1940*, Hamden, CT: Archon, 1990, p. 103-165; Florian Rothbrust, *Guderian's XIXth Panzer Corps and the Battle of France*, New York: Praeger, 1990.

147. See, e.g., Kenneth Pollack, *Arabs at War: Military Effectiveness, 1948-1991*, Lincoln: University of Nebraska Press, 2002; Anthony Cordesman and Abraham Wagner, *The Lessons of Modern War: The Arab-Israeli Conflicts, 1973-1989*, Boulder, CO: Westview, 1990.

148. Assuming 2006 Israeli casualty and Hezbollah strength figures documented above, with strength and casualty figures for 1956, 1967, 1973, and 1982 drawn from J. David Singer and Melvin Small, *Correlates of War Project: International and Civil War Data, 1816-1992* [Computer File], Ann Arbor, MI: Inter-University Consortium for Political and Social Research, 1994.

in conventional war fighting were clearly imperfect in 2006—but they were also well within the observed bounds of other state military actors in the Middle East and elsewhere, and significantly superior to many such states'.

Overall, then, Hezbollah's combination of methods and proficiency places them well to the right of the classical guerrilla model in Figure 1. While they were less "conventional" than, for example, the U.S. defense of Saudi Arabia in 1990, they were probably not significantly less so than other Arab state militaries in Middle Eastern warfare; in terms of their net *proficiency*, they may well have been at least as adept at holding ground, for example, as some European militaries in the 20th century world wars (such as 1940 France or 1941 Italy). On balance, Hezbollah's behavior in 2006 thus places them within a band that includes many state militaries in interstate warfare.

In this sense Hezbollah may be part of a broader emerging trend. A number of nonstate actors have recently displayed military behaviors that appear to incorporate major elements of traditionally "conventional" methods. Al-Qaeda fighters in Afghanistan, for example, made effective use of terrain and man-made works for cover and concealment at Bai Beche and the Shah-i-Kot valley in 2001-02, where they attempted to hold ground against a Coalition offensive in the context of a differentiated theater of war, as did Chechen infantry in Grozny in 1994-95.[149] Rwandan

149. Stephen Biddle, *Afghanistan and the Future of Warfare: Implications for Army and Defense Policy*, Carlisle, PA: Strategic Studies Institute, U.S. Army War College, November 2002, pp. 26-49; *idem*, "Afghanistan and the Future of Warfare," *Foreign Affairs*, Vol. 82, No. 2, March/April 2003, pp. 31-46; Olga Oliker, *Russia's Chechen Wars 1994-2000: Lessons from Urban Combat*, Santa Monica, CA: RAND, 2003; Timothy L. Thomas, "The Battle of Grozny,

rebels in 1994 launched a major offensive that swept government forces from power in about 3 months of combat using methods that some have compared to U.S. Army doctrine for conventional theater warfare.[150] Slovenian, Bosnia, Serbian, and Croatian separatists in the Balkans used uniformed, conventionally-equipped formations to take and hold ground in the 1990s.[151]

More broadly still, a conception of military behavior as a continuum between guerrilla and conventional extremes with most real cases in between implies a more complex, and more challenging, defense planning problem than many transformation advocates assume. The very choice of the term "transformation" implies a need for radical change. And the nature of this radical change usually amounts to a restructuring of the military around a more perfect response to single points on this spectrum.

The original case for high-tech "transformation" as advocated by former Secretary of Defense Donald Rumsfeld, for example, amounted to a program for restructuring around the demands of the classically conventional extreme. That is, the standoff precision strike capabilities on which this program centered

---

Deadly Classroom for Urban Combat," *Parameters*, Vol. 29, No. 2, Summer 1999; Thomas, "The 31 December 1994—8 February 1995 Battle for Grozny," in William G. Robertson and Lawrence A. Yates, eds., *Block by Block: The Challenges of Urban Operations*, Ft. Leavenworth, KS: U.S. Army Command and General Staff College Press, 2003.

150. Defense Intelligence Agency Report, "Rwanda: The Rwandan Patriotic Front's Offensive", May 9, 1994 [accessed at *www.gwu.edu/~nsarchiv/NSAEBB/NSAEBB53/rw050994.pdf* on May 8, 2008]; Donald Jameson, "Missing Pieces of the Rwanda Puzzle," *Washington Times*, May 23, 1994, A20; Donatella Lorch, "Rwanda Rebels: Army of Exiles Fights for a Home," *New York Times*, June 9, 1994, A10.

151. See, esp., Office of Russian and European Analysis, *Balkan Battlegrounds, A Military History of the Yugoslav Conflict, 1990-1995*, 2 vols., Washington, DC: Central Intelligence Agency, 2002.

would be very effective against opponents who present massed targets maneuvering in large formations away from populated areas—in fact, against this kind of enemy, a U.S. force built around standoff precision would be the optimal solution. If the enemy fights this way, to retain large numbers of U.S. dismounted infantry, heavy armor, short-range tube artillery, and other traditional, lower-technology means for close combat would be both less necessary and less tolerable, given their great expense and hence their high opportunity cost against the acquisition of the information infrastructure needed to implement "network-centric" standoff warfare. To retain these artifacts of an older style of fighting represented an unacceptable drain on resources, which would reduce the U.S. military's real combat power against the kind of classically conventional enemy that the high-tech transformation school typically assumed.[152]

---

152. On the high-tech transformation agenda, see, e.g., Donald Rumsfeld, "Transforming the Military," *Foreign Affairs*, May/June 2002; idem, *FY 2007 Defense Budget Statement Before the Senate Appropriations Committee-Defense Subcommittee*, May 17, 2006, available at *www.defenselink.mil/speeches/2006/sp20060517-13063.html*; Richard Andres, Craig Wills, and Thomas Griffith Jr., "Winning With Allies: The Strategic Value of the Afghan Model," *International Security*, Vol. 30, No. 3, Winter 2006, pp. 124-160; Michael Vickers and Robert Martinage, *Revolution in War*, Washington, DC: Center for Strategic and Budgetary Assessments, 2004; Brigadier General David A. Deptula, *Effects-Based Operations: Change in the Nature of Warfare*, Arlington, VA: Aerospace Education Foundation, 2001; Max Boot, "The New American Way of War," *Foreign Affairs*, Vol. 82, No. 4, July/August 2003, pp. 41-58; Jim Mannion, "Rumsfeld Rejects Case for Boosting Size of Army," *Washington Times*, August 6, 2003; Rowan Scarborough, "Decisive Force Now Measured by Speed," *Washington Times*, May 7, 2003; Michael Vickers, *The 2001 Quadrennial Defense Review, the FY 2003 Defense Budget Request and the Way Ahead for Transformation: Meeting the "Rumsfeld Test,"* Washington, DC: Center for Strategic and Budgetary Analysis, June 19, 2002.

But this assumed behavior is a very narrow subset of the range of possibilities, and not necessarily the most likely subset, either. Real enemies often display a blend of classically conventional and more "guerrilla-like" methods. In particular, many real opponents adopt more dispersed, less concentrated, and less exposed defensive dispositions. This may reduce their ability to halt an attack in its tracks at its line of departure, but, in exchange, it provides greater survivability against modern firepower and offers a chance to halt an invasion in depth after an extended period of delay and attrition. Methods of this kind have demonstrated their value against high-firepower opponents repeatedly over the course of modern military history; in fact, the history of tactics and doctrine since 1900 is arguably a story of the gradual discovery of the value of such methods, the spread of this discovery, and its periodic return after episodes of heterodox experimentation.[153] As recently as 2002 in Afghanistan's Shah-i-Kot valley, such methods again proved their utility in reducing the lethality of even 21st century high-firepower, standoff precision strike technology.[154] In fact the utility, persistence, and transnational nature of this intermediate approach to war fighting has led one of us to term it the "modern system," and to argue that it has been essential to battlefield success and failure for over a century of military experience.[155]

To cope with modern-system opponents who use a blend of classically "guerrilla" and classically "conventional" methods, however, requires forces able to close with and defeat opponents whose cover

153. This is the central thesis of Biddle, *Military Power*.

154. See Biddle, *Afghanistan and the Future of Warfare*, pp. 24-43.

155. Biddle, *Military Power*, pp. 2-3.

and concealment make them impossible to destroy at standoff ranges. The legacy military the United States inherited from the Cold War afforded a mix of capabilities—both standoff fires and traditional infantry, armor, and artillery—that enabled it to combine fire and movement and overcome even opponents who mastered enough of the modern system to survive standoff fires alone. This mix of capabilities offered better performance against a modern-system opponent than a revolution in military affairs (RMA) force could provide, but would be less efficient against an exposed, nonmodern-system enemy such as Saddam's Republican Guard. The Republican Guard's exposure meant it could be destroyed by either kind of American military—the legacy force it faced in 1991, or a putative RMA alternative built around standoff precision—but the latter could do so faster, from safer distances, and with smaller U.S. forces. To gain these efficiencies against exposed, massed enemies at the "conventional" extremum, however, the RMA agenda would accept greatly reduced performance against modern system enemies operating nearer the center of the spectrum in Figure 1. Hence the Rumsfeld transformation agenda amounted to a shift away from a legacy force that was optimized against something like a modern system enemy but which had substantial residual capability against an exposed "conventional extreme" enemy to a force focused almost preclusively on the latter.

Today, the new transformation thesis prescribes policies very different than Rumsfeld's, but its approach is similar: it would reoptimize the legacy military around a different point on the military behavior spectrum. In particular, much of the policy agenda associated with the new, low-tech approach to transformation aims to adapt the military to a threat that is expected to be profoundly intermingled with a civilian population, largely indistinguishable from it, largely uninterested in holding ground, very widely dispersed, heavily reliant on roadside bombs, mines, booby traps and other tools for gradual attrition of an occupation force rather than pitched battle, and oriented chiefly toward slow political coercion via the accumulation of cost and unfavorable publicity rather than the use of brute force per se. The low-tech transformation school's preferred tactics, for example, place a premium on restricting the use of violence and distinguishing necessary from unnecessary acts of force; on persistent, widely distributed dismounted presence; and on population control and direct, close interaction with host nation civilians. Its modernization prescriptions emphasize light wheeled vehicles designed for protection against mines and roadside bombs in urban environments. And its organizational and force design prescriptions favor specialties such as military police, civil affairs, military advisory, and special forces, and a buildup of deployable expeditionary civilian interagency capacity, over branches such as armor, artillery, combat engineers, or mechanized infantry.[156]

These prescriptions would indeed improve U.S. military performance against classical guerrilla opponents. But they would also reduce it against other opponents who adopt a more intermediate position on the military behavioral spectrum.

Some military fundamentals would apply equally regardless: whomever it expects to fight, the U.S. Army will need to train for safe, accurate small arms marksmanship, disciplined control of fires and use of communications, secure movement in urban environments, first aid, casualty evacuation, and

156. See the references in note 6 above.

a range of other basic skills. But not all skills are readily transferable across modes of warfare or kinds of opponent. As the new Army and Marine Corps counterinsurgency doctrine emphasizes, an important subset of tactics, techniques, and procedures that are essential for effectiveness in battle against uniformed opponents who stand and fight in defense of ground are actively counterproductive against enemies who melt into the population and rely on hit-and-run sniping, ambush, roadside bombs, and assassinations instead.[157] In general, the techniques for rapid decisive application of firepower that are often crucial to survival against "conventional" opponents tend to create more problems than they solve in counterinsurgency. Methods such as large-scale combined arms maneuver, tight synchronization of movement and indirect fire support, tank gunnery from moving platforms, evasive movement drills for armored vehicles, passage of lines, assault breach of barrier systems, or opposed river crossings, to name just a few, play limited roles in counterinsurgency or counterguerrilla warfare.

Similarly, some equipment requirements cut across mission types and warfare styles, but others do not. Some form of protected mobility, for example, is essential regardless; rotary wing transportation and precision fire support are essential regardless; unmanned aerial vehicles for reconnaissance and strike are increasingly valuable whoever the opponent. But other modernization programs are less broadly applicable: lightly armored wheeled vehicles designed chiefly for protection against roadside bombs in

---

157. *Field Manual 3-24, Counterinsurgency*, Washington, DC: Headquarters, Department of the Army, 2007, pp. I-148 to I-157; see also Eliot Cohen, Conrad Crane, Jan Horvath, John Nagl, "Principles, Imperatives, and Paradoxes of Counterinsurgency," *Military Review*, March/April 2006, pp. 2-6.

urban patrolling, for example, would be much less useful for leading an opposed advance against long-range ATGMs up a rural approach route such as the Saluqi valley in Lebanon. And whereas combat unit organizations such as infantry brigades are broadly applicable across a variety of missions and opponents, others, such as large-scale military police, civil affairs, or military advisor formations are more specialized for conflicts against classical guerrilla opponents and less capable in classical conventional warfare.

Real tradeoffs are thus unavoidable. There are only so many training hours in a day, there are only so many soldiers in the Army, and there is only so much money in the Defense budget. If the Army chooses to spend training time on assault breaches of defended minefields, this is time it cannot spend improving soldiers' ability to prevent escalation of violence at an urban checkpoint. If the Army chooses to expand the military police and create a new military advisory corps, the people involved will not be serving in tank battalions. If the United States spends money on Mine Resistant Armor Protected (MRAP) vehicles, this money will not be spent on main battle tanks. It is impossible in the real world of constrained resources and finite time to excel at everything simultaneously. If the U.S. military actually tries to be "pentathletes," as former Army Chief of Staff Peter Schoomaker famously put it,[158] then it is going to have to accept that in real wars against single-event specialists, it may not produce a gold-medal-equivalent performance: pentathletes rarely, if ever, win Olympic gold in any of the single events that make up the pentathlon.

---

158. Sally Donnelly and Douglas Waller, "Ten Questions for General Schoomaker," *Time*, April 22, 2005; Lieutenant Colonel Michael Negard, "Schoomaker: Army Must Fight in 4 Quadrants," *Army News Service*, November 22, 2005.

"Balance" thus cannot mean simultaneous maximum proficiency at everything—this is impossible. And balance in the manner of real pentathletes, who accept less-than-maximum performance in *each* component event in order to avoid catastrophic weakness in any one of them, has not been the U.S. military's choice for at least the last 30 years of its history. On the contrary, the U.S. military's recent tradition has been closer to that of a single-event specialist (and gold medal winner, as it were) in modern-system major warfare. Transformation advocates, effectively, propose a different choice of single-event specialization, but it is not possible to do this without reducing performance for the old event. There is no such thing as a military that can be simultaneously ideal for all opponent types.[159]

---

159. Similar questions have been debated in Israel since the 1990s, and this debate has yielded a sizeable literature. See, e.g., Sergio Catignani, *Israeli Counter-Insurgency and the Intifadas: Dilemmas of a Conventional Army*, New York: Routledge, 2008; Martin van Creveld, *The Sword and the Olive: A Critical History of the Israeli Defence Force*, New York: Public Affairs, 1998; Stuart A. Cohen, *Israel and its Army: Continuity and Change*, New York: Routledge, 2008; Emanuel Wald, *The Wald Report: The Decline of Israeli National Security Since 1967*, Boulder, CO: Westview Press, 1992; Stuart A. Cohen, "The Israel Defense Force: Continuity and Change," in Barry Rubin and Thomas A. Keaney eds., *Armed Forces in the Middle East: Politics and Strategy*, London: Frank Cass, 2002; Eliot Cohen, Michael J. Eisenstadt, Andrew Bacevich, *Knives, Tanks, and Missiles: Israel's Security Revolution*, Washington, DC: Washington Institute for Near East Policy, 1998; Uri Bar-Joseph, ed., *Israel's National Security Towards the 21st Century*, New York: Routledge, 2001; Clive Jones, "Israeli Counter-Insurgency Strategy and the War in South Lebanon, 1985-97," *Small Wars and Insurgencies*, Vol. 8, No. 3, Winter 1997, pp. 82-108; Gabriel Ben-Dor, Ami Pedahzur, and Badi Hasisi, "Israel's National Security Doctrine under Strain: The Crisis of the Reserve Army," *Armed Forces & Society*, Vol. 28, No. 2, Winter 2002, pp. 233-255. For discussions of how Israeli defense policy has reflected this debate

This, however, poses serious challenges for U.S. policy makers in light of the tension between the implications of the 2006 Lebanon campaign and the demands of Iraq and Afghanistan. Ongoing operations in Iraq and Afghanistan demand maximum capability for defeating current enemies who practice a close approximation of classical guerrilla warfare; Lebanon suggests a possibility for future enemies who could wage war more conventionally than this. The different demands of these different styles of fighting thus leave defense planners with a dilemma: the United States cannot simultaneously maximize its potential for both, but neither prospect can safely be ignored, requiring a painful choice in which something important must be sacrificed whichever choice one makes.

By contrast, many in today's future warfare debate see a simpler, less conflicted picture. It is now widely argued that the future is one of nonstate opponents who will use asymmetric, irregular methods much like those of today's Iraqi or Afghan insurgents. If so, then there is little or no real, meaningful risk in transforming the U.S. military around the needs of

---

in recent years, see, e.g., Ben David, "Extensive Cuts to Hit Israeli Ground Forces the Most," *Jane's Defence Weekly*, July 16, 2003; Ben-David, "All Quiet on the Eastern Front, so Israel will Revise IDF Organization and Doctrine," *Jane's Defence Weekly*, March 1, 2004; Ben-David, "Israel Set to Restructure Ground Forces," *Jane's Defence Weekly*, March 10, 2004; Ben-David, "Israel's Low-Intensity Conflict Doctrine," *Jane's Defence Weekly*, September 1, 2004; Catignani, "Israel Defence Forces Organizational Changes in an Era of Budgetary Cutbacks," *RUSI Journal*, October 2004, pp. 72-76; Ben-David, "Debriefing Teams Brand IDF Doctrine 'Completely Wrong'"; Ben-David, "Israel Reflects—New Model Army?"; Ben-David, "IDF Shifts Focus to Ground Forces," *Jane's Defence Weekly*, January 10, 2007; Ben-David, "IDF Unveils Five-Year Plan to Boost Capabilities," *Jane's Defence Weekly*, September 12, 2007; Allison Krant, "Multi-Year Plan to Strengthen IDF Conventional Capabilities," *JINSA Online*, November 12, 2007.

the guerrilla end of the behavioral spectrum. On the contrary, this would unambiguously improve U.S. national security by reshaping the military to meet the real needs of the future, finally shedding the inherited baggage of a Cold War force whose bureaucratic inertia had thwarted needed change until now. The particular policy agenda associated with this view is diametrically opposite the Rumsfeld transformation program, but perhaps ironically it shares Rumsfeld's frustration with the perceived inertia and apparently old-fashioned thinking of the institutional military and its defenders of conventional war making capacity, and it shares Rumsfeld's insistence on transformational change in light of this. If the future really is one of nonstate actors waging an information-age version of classical guerrilla warfare, then the low-tech transformation agenda is an unambiguous good, and the defense planning challenge of today and tomorrow is a politically demanding but intellectually straightforward matter of pushing hard enough to get a resistant bureaucracy to do the right thing and accept as much irregular warfare transformation as it can be made to swallow.

The Lebanon experience, however, suggests a future of less clarity and more diversity. Lebanon in 2006 shows us a concrete example of a nonstate actor whose military behavior was far from the classical guerrilla model seen in today's Iraq and Afghanistan. And Hezbollah in 2006 is unlikely to be the last of these—other nonstate actors elsewhere appear to be adopting similarly rightward positions on Figure 1's taxonomy of military behavior. It cannot yet be known how broad this trend may be, what its root causes are, or how far it will go—to answer these questions is a critical research requirement for the defense intellectual community today. But Hezbollah does demonstrate, unambiguously, that even today's nonstate actors are not limited to the irregular, guerrilla-model military methods so often assumed in the future warfare debate.

And this means that today's defense planning challenge is more complex than the current debate often implies. There are real risks both in changing too little *and* in changing too much. And to avert failure in Iraq or Afghanistan may require a real sacrifice in meeting future challenges elsewhere that cannot be avoided by ignoring conventional threats or by insisting on balance. The tradeoffs are real, they are not artificial, and the dilemmas they create cannot be ducked.

This certainly does *not* mean that the United States should return to a preclusive focus on major warfare as it did before 2003—or that a Hezbollah threat should replace the Red Army in the Fulda Gap as the focus for U.S. defense planning. Single-event (or single-threat) specialization in a world where we could face multiple events (or multiple threats) is dangerous whichever event one would choose. The pre-2003 U.S. military was very close to this degree of specialization for modern-system enemies; while it enjoyed more residual capability against other foes than an RMA force would have, this residual proved inadequate against the guerrilla opposition we faced increasingly beginning in 2004. And it would be dangerous and unwise to return to the pre-2003 focus and accept the degree of unpreparedness for guerrilla methods this produced.

Nor does this analysis imply that we should accept failure in Iraq or Afghanistan so as to rebalance the military toward more conventional enemies than we face there. Failure in either Iraq or Afghanistan could have grave consequences for U.S. national interests.

Until these theaters are stabilized—or unless stability becomes infeasible—it will be essential to maximize U.S. performance in these ongoing wars even if this reduces future potential for some as-yet unseen war elsewhere. The analysis of Lebanon above thus does not presuppose appropriate U.S. policy for Iraq or Afghanistan.[160]

What an analysis of Lebanon can do, however, is to show the limits of some prominent analyses of future warfare and to highlight the true dilemmas associated with defense policy decisionmaking. The future is not simply one of guerrilla-like warfare by nonstate actors. And this means that a thoroughgoing transformation to suit the demands of such warfare has real risks and real dangers as well as benefits. It may still be the right policy to shift the U.S. military's focus

160. In particular, while policy failure in a future conflict against a conventionally capable nonstate actor would be bad, failure in Iraq or Afghanistan could be worse; it might simply be necessary to pay the price in military preparedness for an unknown future in order to avoid failure in a known present. In general, the problem of U.S. policy in Iraq and Afghanistan has long been one of picking the least-bad option from among an unattractive menu of choices. And like everything else about Iraq and Afghanistan, the problem of designing the military that will wage these wars, and also meet other threats elsewhere, is one of balancing costs and risks on all sides of the ledger. What Lebanon in 2006 shows is that these costs and risks are indeed real: even nonstate enemies will not necessarily limit themselves to irregular warfare. For a more detailed discussion of the dilemmas of policy choice in Iraq, see Stephen Biddle, "Stabilizing Iraq from the Bottom Up," Testimony Before the Committee on Foreign Relations, United States Senate, Second Session, 110th Congress, April 2, 2008; idem, "Patient Stabilized?" *The National Interest*, March/April 2008, pp. 19-25; *idem*, "Evaluating Options for Partial Withdrawals from Iraq," Testimony Before the House Armed Services Committee Subcommittee on Oversight and Investigations in *Alternatives for Iraq, Hearings Before the Committee on Armed Services, U.S. House of Representatives,* One Hundred Tenth Congress, First Session, July 25, 2007.

toward guerrilla warfare, especially relative to the pre-2003 military's radical avoidance of this problem. It may even be the right policy to make a radical shift toward counterguerrilla proficiency if this is the only way to avoid defeat in such wars. Or it may not: an analysis of Lebanon per se cannot establish how much counterguerrilla capability is enough. But to make this decision requires a sound understanding of the costs—as well as the benefits—of all the options. And a true reoptimization of the military for classical guerrilla warfare would entail real costs in a world where Hezbollah-like enemies may become more common over time. There is no escaping this tradeoff via a simple projection of a monolithic future threat, and one need not necessarily be a bureaucratic obstructionist to worry about non-guerrilla enemies. What Hezbollah in 2006 shows is that in defense planning, as in economics, there is no such thing as a free lunch or an unambiguous, risk-free policy. The real world is one of tradeoffs, and all options have downsides—even the options that look most forward-thinking.

www.ingramcontent.com/pod-product-compliance
Ingram Content Group UK Ltd.
Pitfield, Milton Keynes, MK11 3LW, UK
UKHW041934190726
13854UKWH00004B/1585

9 781257 128785